GLOBALIZATION AND MARKETIZATION OF GOVERNMENT SERVICES

Also by Andrew Massey

MANAGING THE PUBLIC SECTOR: A Comparative Analysis of the
United Kingdom and the United States

TECHNOCRATS AND NUCLEAR POLITICS

Globalization and Marketization of Government Services

Comparing Contemporary Public Sector Developments

Edited by

Andrew Massey
School of Social and Historical Studies
University of Portsmouth

First published in Great Britain 1997 by
MACMILLAN PRESS LTD
Houndmills, Basingstoke, Hampshire RG21 6XS and London
Companies and representatives throughout the world

A catalogue record for this book is available from the British Library.

ISBN 0–333–65409–9

First published in the United States of America 1997 by
ST. MARTIN'S PRESS, INC.,
Scholarly and Reference Division,
175 Fifth Avenue, New York, N.Y. 10010

ISBN 0–312–17520–5

Library of Congress Cataloging-in-Publication Data
Globalization and marketization of government services : comparing
contemporary public sector developments / edited by Andrew Massey.
p.   cm.
Includes bibliographical references and index.
ISBN 0–312–17520–5 (cloth)
1. Organizational change.   2. Contracting out.   3. Privatization.
4. Public administration.   5. Comparative government.   I. Massey,
Andrew, 1958–   .
JF1525.O73G56 1997
352.3—dc21   97–5894
                                                                              CIP

This book is printed on paper suitable for recycling and made from fully managed and
sustained forest sources.

10   9   8   7   6   5   4   3   2   1
06   05   04   03   02   01   00   99   98   97

Printed in Great Britain by
The Ipswich Book Company Ltd
Ipswich, Suffolk

Contents

Preface and Acknowledgements

There has been a global revolution in the delivery of public services. The dynamics for change have been fashionable new ideas and powerful new technologies. Throughout the world, governments of all ideological persuasions have transformed the way in which they approach the implementation of policy. In many cases activities traditionally associated with public provision, via the existence of a welfare state, have been privatized or contracted out to private sector providers, many of whom are part of multinational corporations beyond the governmental control of any one nation state. This raises fundamental questions regarding the role of government, the ability of governments to deliver on election promises, the way in which a country's executive may be held to account for the implementation of its policy decisions, and the development of academic analysis to more fully understand these changes.

The perspective adopted by this book, is to discuss these aspects of change and their implications by first exploring some of the new concepts used and questioning their applicability. The book then uses case studies and some comparative examples to explore the theoretical issues further, before concluding with a discussion of the utility and academic impact of the bureau-shaping model.

The chapter by Massey begins by exploring the attempts to define new managerial and policy paradigms in terms of globalization, and whether there may be said to be a new global paradigm. It then examines the European focus on new public management, contrasting it with American concerns over reinventing government in terms of a post-bureaucratic reform paradigm. Dunleavy's chapter develops these themes through a sophisticated discussion on the nature and possible effects of marketizing government services. He applies a complex analytical framework to the issues raised by the evolution of a global market in government services. It is a market, however, which also often lacks the necessary political structure for ensuring democratic accountability in the provision of those services. He explores the loss of national administrative control which may result from the contracting out of so much government activity, applying the bureau-shaping model in his argument that top-level officials often have no inherent interest in management, or in expanding the size of their budgets or total staff, preferring to concentrate on protecting the privileges and status of their office.

In her first chapter, Margetts evaluates the National Performance Review in the USA, outlining its development and what she calls a more humanist version of New Public Management. Her chapter charts the different dynamics and pressures, from the pluralist American political system, upon the Clinton administration's attempt at fundamental bureaucratic reform, after the years of malign neglect under Republican administrations. Goldsmith analyses the impact of the Europeanization of government and the new regional, if not global thinking which permeates and disaggregates policy making in the European Union. His chapter clearly indicates the lacuna, or democratic deficit, which lies at the heart of much criticism of supranational decision making, especially when it is combined with marketization. This point is returned to by Margetts in her second chapter, albeit in a modified form, where she provides a case study in marketization; the withdrawal by the British government from information technology development and its radical outsourcing on long contracts to predominantly American private sector providers.

Jordan's chapter delivers a magisterial rebuke to the gurus of reinventing and re-engineering government. He makes the plausible case for maintaining older bureaucratic systems on the grounds that they were first established to overcome the deficiencies of inefficient or corrupt regimes. Their wholesale replacement by a new order is a process, he argues, which lacks democratic debate and is based on spurious empirical research. Cope, in his chapter, argues many of these reforms are based on the obvious impact of budget-maximizing models which began to become influential in North America in the early 1970s, being slowly developed until their ideas swept across the globe in the late 1980s and early 1990s. He returns to Dunleavy's bureau-shaping model to assess these changes from a comparative perspective and finishes by noting the theoretical advances the model has given to academics, while questioning how much further it may be developed.

A research seminar at the University of Portsmouth, on Market Testing for government services, supported by the Public Administration Committee of the Joint University Council, provided the forum for earlier drafts of the chapters by Dunleavy and Jordan. Dunleavy also acknowledges the comments and suggestions of contributors to a seminar of the universities of Strathclyde, Glasgow Caledonian, and Stirling, and another seminar at the University of Sheffield. Earlier versions of the chapters by Dunleavy and Jordan appeared in *Public Policy and Administration*, Volume 9 Number 2, and the chapter by Jordan appeared in *Public Administration*, Volume 72 Number 2. A version of Chapter 5 appeared in *Public Policy and Administration*, Volume

10 Number 3. All are updated and reproduced here with the kind permission of the editors of those journals.

I would like to thank Patrick Dunleavy, Trevor Smith of the University of Ulster, and Sylvia Horton of the University of Portsmouth, for their comments on an earlier version of Chapter 1. Finally, the editors at Macmillan and Patrick Dunleavy of the LSE were a fund of constructive and supportive ideas for this book; they deserve and have my profound gratitude.

Andrew Massey
University of Portsmouth

Notes on the Contributors

Stephen Cope is Principal Lecturer in Policy Studies at the University of Portsmouth.

Patrick Dunleavy is Professor of Government at the London School of Economics and Political Science.

Michael Goldsmith is Professor of Government at the University of Salford.

Grant Jordan is Professor of Politics at the University of Aberdeen.

Helen Margetts is Lecturer in Politics at Birkbeck College, the University of London.

Andrew Massey is Reader in Public Policy at the University of Portsmouth.

1 In Search of the State: Markets, Myths and Paradigms

Andrew Massey

> So the Lord scattered them abroad from thence upon the face of all the earth: and they left of to build the city. Therefore is the name of it called Babel; because the Lord did there confound the language of all the earth: and from thence did the Lord scatter them abroad upon the face of the earth. (Genesis, 11, 5–9)

> Rather than a thousand shoots blossoming into as many different flowering plants, mankind will come to seem like a long wagon train strung out along a road ... The apparent differences in the situations of the wagons will not be seen as reflecting permanent and necessary differences between the people riding in the wagons, but simply a product of their different positions along the road. (Fukuyama, 1992, pp. 338–9)

TRANSITIONAL TIMES

We are living through a time of transition. For some observers the human race is entering its 'Global Age'; it is a perilous, often undemocratic journey which cannot be shunned, but must be navigated with trepidation and care. The globalization of markets and money, politics and people is imbued with fearsome ambiguity. It is a period in which the nation state may be in terminal decline, yet there is a simultaneous rebirth of atavistic, often bloody nationalism. Analysing the thesis and antithesis of global integration versus national sovereignty is the praxis of the age.

Adherents to an alternative perspective point to the relative novelty of the nation state, arguing its modern expression, as a monopoly of sovereignty within a geographically defined region, may be traced to the seventeenth century (Hirst and Thompson, 1995, pp. 408–9). Furthermore, analysts of both the left and the right question the global theorists' belief that national economies are being subsumed by a global economy, with all its subsequent political and cultural ramifications, and suggest the world economy remains an *international* system and the nation state retains a pivotal political role (ibid.; Goldsmith, 1995).

What cannot be denied, however, is that the nature of governmental institutions, the functions they carry out and the manner in which these roles are performed, have been subjected to an unprecedented series of changes throughout the world since the early 1980s. The dynamic for this change has come from:

- technical innovation;
- an attempt at the paradigmatic redefinition of the role of the state and state organisations;
- the development of treaty-based supranational institutions;
- the perceived threats by some countries to their national sovereignty/security caused by the rapid economic advances of their competitors (Tolchin, 1996, pp. 1–8).

Many of these aspects are fully discussed in subsequent chapters of this book. By way of preparing the ground for these discussions, however, the rest of this chapter will explore what is meant by changes in the paradigm of state agencies, discuss what are the core competencies of the state, and note the perceived 'democratic deficit' inherent to supranational organizations.

METAPHORS AND PARADIGMS

The corpus of philosophical and social science literature engaged with the ontological and epistemological problems of understanding the relationship, and relative roles, of the state and society is vast and continually expanding. The concern of this book, that is public administration and public management, is one small segment of the total. But even this sub-discipline of the social sciences is beset with analysis attempting to make sense of an alleged paradigmatic shift experienced by practitioners and closely monitored by their academic observers (Overman and Boyd, 1994; Campbell and Wilson, 1995; Hood, 1995). It has been generally accepted within contemporary social science that 'reality' is socially constructed (Berger and Luckmann, 1966). The abstractions by which the very structures of social and political activity are implemented and understood, such as 'money', 'the state', 'authority' and 'legitimacy', are subjective constructions. As Berger and Luckmann argue:

> The insight into the dialectic between social reality and individual existence in history is by no means new. It was, of course, most powerfully introduced into modern social thought by Marx. (1966, p. 209)

Furthermore:

> Subjective reality is thus always dependent upon specific plausibility structures, that is, the specific social base and social processes required

for its maintenance. One can maintain one's self-identification as a man of importance only in a milieu that confirms this identity; one can maintain one's Catholic faith only if one retains one's significant relationship with the Catholic community; and so forth. (ibid., p. 174)

These constructions vary over time and place and find abstract expression in a specific context as paradigms. Models or 'ideal types' are employed as tools to aid understanding of these paradigms. That is, a way to make sense of the policy process is to use meta-analysis, which Parsons explains as:

understanding the idea that the analysis of public policy proceeds by employing metaphors: we analyze by describing something in terms of something else. Public policy, as other forms of political analysis, uses metaphors or models as devices to explore the 'unknown' and possibly unknowable world of politics. (1995, p. 1)

In this century the analysis of politics and public administration has proceeded through employing a set of changing and often contradictory metaphors, models and paradigms.

The generally accepted definition of a paradigm is Kuhn's; a paradigm is:

the entire constellation of beliefs, values, techniques and so on shared by members of a given community. (1970, p. 175)

Although this explanation is taken from his study of scientific paradigms and the method by which progress is made within the scientific communities, it has a wider, almost universal appeal. Given the nature of social science, there will be a number of communities, and therefore a number of paradigms, in existence at any given time.

Parsons discusses a sophisticated list of paradigms, approaches and metaphors to the study of the policy process, noting Guba's four main paradigms of social enquiry as:

- positivism;
- post-positivism;
- critical theory;
- constructivism (Parsons, 1995, p. 71).

While a healthy, sceptical, indeed heuristic approach to analysis strongly suggests one ought not to accept any framework uncritically, Guba's typology is almost a chronology, charting the shift within social science from primitive empiricism to the constructivist perspective which sees reality as mental constructs with relevance only to those who hold them and any others affected by their actions (ibid.). From out of this typology may be extrapolated the two views most commonly discussed in current public administration literature, the Weberian bureaucratic paradigm, which is largely a critical theory approach, and the rational choice/economic approach to administration known as New Public Management (NPM), which is largely a positivist perspective. The irony here is that in economics at least the rational choice approach had been largely discredited by the time it began to be applied by writers such as Niskanen (1971, 1973; see also Dunleavy, 1991) to the political arena as Public Choice theory (Campbell and Wilson, 1995, pp. 304–6). Yet it is this paradigm, sometimes referred to as a sub-set of the post-bureaucratic reform paradigm (Overman and Boyd, 1994; Massey, 1995a) that has ousted the old-style Weberian model, in its various manifestations, in a large number of Western democracies over the last two decades.

PARADIGMS AND NEW PUBLIC MANAGEMENT

Both the evidence for globalization *per se* in public management, however, and the notion of a new global paradigm may be questioned (Hood, 1995, pp. 104–16). Indeed, a careful review of the evidence may suggest the policy analyst is best served by adopting a sceptical view regarding the case that an 'old' paradigm or model ever really existed. For example, Hood argues:

> It is easy to be carried away by grand claims of historical inevitability and global convergence on some new epoch-making paradigm … [but] … such claims should be treated with scepticism. Certainly there does seem to have been a movement away from the doctrines of the Progressive era public administration in several OECD states. And undoubtedly some managerial catchwords have such a wide currency that one can speak of a new global vocabulary. (ibid., p. 105)

But it is more doubtful, he surmises, that there is such a thing as a new global paradigm. He cites three reasons:

- it has not been adequately demonstrated that a retreat from old-style public administration will inevitably lead to a worldwide acceptance of any single style of new management to replace it;
- the concept of a new global paradigm ignores the 'very different and typically "path dependent" local agendas to which contemporary public management changes are responding. Where the same thing is happening, it is often for quite different reasons, reflecting different underlying political agendas';

- the belief that some kind of 'stable' new structure is being implemented globally overplays 'the elements of continuity in contemporary public management change' and downplays 'the typically self-disequilibrating capacity of public management doctrines as a result of the unintended effects they produce' (ibid., pp. 105–6).

Furthermore, to speak of a global shift from one paradigm to another is to assume 'that there is a single old paradigm and a single exit route from it' (ibid.). Hood suggests that although many states acquired a public administration which bore common aspects and could, therefore, be labelled as being part of the same old global model, for example, the populist reforms in the US, the Weberian model in various European countries or the British Northcote-Trevelyan/Haldane model, in fact each reflected the peculiar historical, cultural and political context in which it was situated.

Although there were common elements to those countries which followed the Westminster/Whitehall model and they in turn had some commonality with states which adopted versions of the old Roman/Napoleonic code and they accordingly had something in common with those which adopted a populist/federal structure, there remained great differences which resulted from the unique historical experience of the state involved. Each country constructed its public administration in order to achieve different aims in the light of the perceived problems (the perceived reality) of its political elites. Globally, therefore, this is not so much a paradigm as a propensity, almost a fashion. The paradigm, if it may be labelled as such, exists within the individual state.

Despite their catchy sub-heading ('Death of a Paradigm?'), Campbell and Wilson (1995, pp. 98–248) follow a similar track in emphasizing the importance of context for understanding the old public administrative structures and new public management[1] structures in Western countries, although they rightly excoriate those foolish enough to argue that comparison across disparate systems is so meaningless as to be futile. Perhaps their subheading should be 'Dramatic Reform of a Model', given their evidence of a lack of coherent logical reform within the UK, in contrast to the efforts of New Zealand's reformers to put into place 'an entire theoretical apparatus – based on Public Choice and principal/agent theory' (ibid., p. 244). In Britain the administrative reforms have tended to raise more questions than to provide answers, especially with regard to the accountability of the executive to the legislature (and the electorate) and within the executive hierarchies (ibid., pp. 249–50; Massey, 1995a).

This reflects the attempt by British ministers and senior civil servants to combine those elements from the old bureaucratic system with the aspects of NPM which most appeal to them, an attempt clearly visible in two recent Government White Papers on the future of the civil service (Cabinet Office, 1994, Cm 2627; 1995, Cm 2748; Massey, 1995b). Hood argues that any system which attempts to effect such a convergence in order to attain this most difficult of hybrids is unlikely to succeed due to each approach 'involving an underlying logic which, if taken to its limits, will tend to destroy all the others' (1995, p. 111). It is unlikely the British executive will prove as logical as Hood, but will continue instead to employ a Lindblomian (1979) approach to muddling through in the hope of reconciling the unreconcilable.

A quizzical approach to the argument that there is such a thing as a post-bureaucratic reform paradigm, is attempted by Overman and Boyd (1994) which presumably assumes there is (or was) a bureaucratic or even pre-bureaucratic reform paradigm, as informed by the best practice research model of writers like Osborne and Gaebler (1993) with their pretensions to reinventing government.[2] Overman and Boyd argue best practice research tends toward an 'in-crowd' of reforming managers, does not accumulate practice wisdom, and its practices are not transferable. In short, it lacks the scientific approach required of good social science in that it is not theory testing research and is insufficiently critical and insufficiently probing (1994, pp. 76–86). If there are any universal laws of management they remain to be discovered (Massey, 1993). For example, the argument that much of the current work defines paradigm so broadly that the word is 'drained of meaning' (Hood, 1995) appears powerful, though perhaps overstates the case. It may instead be argued that at any time there are several paradigms in operation and that they are variations taken from the aforementioned typology provided by Guba.

The dynamics of change reflect the competition, even conflict, this provides both inter- and intranationally. Similarly, social science models of analysis are derived from, but are not necessarily synonymous with these paradigms. A conscientious researcher will apply several models of analysis to each policy area in order to extract the maximum understanding (Dunleavy, 1986). To argue that the shift to forms of NPM is more akin to a fashion driven by political expediency and technological innovation, rather than a paradigmatic shift in the entire constellation of fundamental beliefs, values and techniques shared by members of a given community, to return to Kuhn's definition, is not to deny common global elements, simply to assert that the new global paradigm is not as global, fundamental or paradigmatic as some observers would argue. It is competing, in any given context, with one or more paradigms because there will be one or more communities, groups or elites operating within the national and global policy process. They in turn will apply a heuristic approach to the tools of modern management and administration, applying them eclectically to the 'real' problems by which they feel themselves beset, usually irrespective of the ideological stable from which they come. Concrete examples here are the transformations wrought upon their respective public sectors by the Labour parties of New Zealand and Australia (Campbell and Wilson, 1995).

Whether or not it may be called a paradigm, NPM, however, retains a powerful influence upon the workings of the state and the concrete manifestation of fashionable new techniques, such as outsourcing and downsizing will have a profound and long-lasting impact on the ability of governments to deliver their manifesto pledges, or indeed to control the provision and mode of delivery of state services, as well as the collection of resources. There is a fundamental fiduciary and accountability aspect to be explored that has been neglected by policy makers and policy analysts alike. Dunleavy's chapter in this book makes an important contribution towards that debate.

COMMON THEMES AND CORE COMPETENCIES

Some themes which have now become common currency to students of public administration were highlighted in Hood's inaugural lecture, where he tracked what he termed some 'administrative megatrends'. British observers began to use the term 'New Public Management' as a shorthand for many of the new trends in public administration. While NPM is still not so readily used in the USA, where the terms 'reinventing government' and 'post-bureaucratic reform paradigm' are more often heard, in Europe NPM is increasingly utilized to explain an attempt to redefine administrative culture and structures. For some observers these attempts at a cultural reform are a collection of global megatrends, which Hood argues are:

- attempts by many governments to check the growth of government;
- the internationalization of public administration;
- automation in public administration;
- the privatization of public administration;
- the rise of the new public management (1990, p. 4).

Since that lecture these trends have become more pronounced. The rise of NPM in particular has proved seemingly inexorable, although attempts to check the growth of government, privatization, automation and indeed the internationalization of public administration may all be seen to be adjuncts to, or elements of, NPM. Hood contends the 'thrust of NPM's doctrines is a familiar litany' and includes:

- an emphasis away from issues of policy to those of management and quantifiable methods of performance;
- a disaggregated approach to management of the public sector which includes the break-up of traditional bureaucratic structures and attempts to increase competition within the public sector;
- a strong emphasis on cost-cutting, often through the use of private sector business techniques;
- a general adoption of private sector corporate practices and a deregulation of government in favour of market approaches (ibid., pp. 9–10).

In many Western countries the implementation of NPM techniques has led to a dramatic increase in the agencification, marketization and privatization of the public sector. But it must be noted that the implementation has not followed the same pattern in all cases. The experience of Australasia is markedly different to that of the UK, which is itself different to that of the rest of the EU, Canada or the US (Campbell and Wilson, 1995; Hood, 1995; Pollitt, 1995). Even agencification varies considerably, and agencies may be said to be situated along a continuum, as identified in Table 1.1, which varies according to the context of each example. That is, the role of the agency, the political and cultural context in which it is situated and the prevailing political ethos of the state of which it forms a part. The position of agencies on the continuum, therefore, is not fixed, indeed in some cases it may be positively volatile, such as when a largely autonomous agency becomes embroiled in scandal and has to be reined-in by elected politicians. With an example like this the agency would move from left to right along the continuum fairly rapidly, but would be likely to regain some of its former position once remedial action had been taken.

Table 1.1: Agency Model: a Simplified Continuum

Autarky	*Cypher*
Fully autonomous agencies	Purely executive agencies
Judicial agencies	British Next Steps agencies

Source: Based on Massey 1995b, p. 176.

NPM clearly encourages agencification and thereby a more fluid, less structured public sector. Indeed, the boundaries between the public and private sectors merge into a penumbra of contractorization and contractor principal/agent relationships. This is sometimes referred to as the hollowing-out of the state and may lead to a move back to a nightwatchman state or to its twenty-first century equivalent, the enabling state (Stewart, 1992; Rhodes, 1995).

The earlier definitions of NPM have been continually refined and updated. NPM, it could be argued, may now be seen to seek:

- the reduction of bureaucratic rules and hierarchies;
- budget transparency and to identify the costs of inputs and outputs;
- the use of a network of contracts rather than fiduciary relationships;
- to disaggregate organizations and their functions, introducing purchaser/provider distinctions;
- to increase provider competition;
- to increase consumer power through enhanced scope for exit and redress (Dunleavy and Hood, 1994, p. 9; Hood, 1994, p. 130).

There are close links here with Overman and Boyd's definition of the post-bureaucratic reform 'paradigm', which they argue is:

- anticipatory;
- strategic;
- results directed;
- based on executive leadership (rather than explicitly political leadership);
- market oriented;
- customer driven;
- entrepreneurial (1994, p. 75).

While there are several key concepts that appear to have a global application, namely those relating to markets, individualism and measurable performance indicators, it is hard to accept this positivistic set of criteria as a new paradigm. It is, however, a shift in the *model* used for structuring state organizations, a move away from the rule-governed hierarchies informed by Weberian critical theory, hierarchies designed to provide more than simple justice, fiduciary scrupulousness and equity of provision, but also to engage in symbolic, almost ritualistic state activity, engaging the support of the public and garnering legitimacy for the state.

The switch to NPM and the loss of these symbolic legitimizing functions has had some severely negative effects upon public support for state institutions across North America and the EU. Even though reforms have been implemented under the banner of ideological liberalism, the negative legitimacy effects being manifested have appalled some influential ideological liberals who have despaired of the New Right (Gray, 1993, 1996; Goldsmith, 1995). Goldsmith has gone so far as to note that much of the globalization and liberalization of the economy, and by implication the accompanying political reforms, has meant that the citizens of Western and Northern

Europe, in his view, are now being made to serve the economy, whereas he argues it is the economy which ought to serve Europe's citizens (Goldsmith, 1995, pp.15–25). The efficiency seeking, cost-cutting logic of modern private sector business techniques and the concomitant dynamics of NPM, however, push towards ever-greater marketization and provision of formally public goods and services via multinational companies operating in the global market.

Like NPM, the old bureaucratic model has many varieties. As noted in the foregoing sections it manifested itself in different ways for different reasons in different states, but its essential elements consist of:

- an impersonal hierarchy of officials who are governed by rules and regulations;
- the officials are appointed to post as a full-time career;
- there is a clear and unimpeachable separation between the private life of officials and their public office;
- officials tend towards specialization;
- the officials are accountable to elected politicians.

Much of this is based on the ideal type constructed by Weber (1946; also Parsons, 1995, pp. 272–3). It may be argued that NPM with its flattened hierarchies, reliance on contracts, individual initiatives and managerial techniques taken from the private sector, is designed to annul the perceived inefficiencies and ineffectiveness of the old system with its concentration upon legal-rational rules, clear lines of accountability, objective implementation of policy and careful scrutiny of all policy options.

What tends to be forgotten by the advocates of NPM is that the complex and often burdensome hierarchies and structures of old-style bureaucracy were established in order to correct the nepotism, injustice, unaccountability and corruption of the systems they replaced. Whether it was the unfettered spoils system of the US which so offended the populists, the corruption of Tory England which provoked the Whigs, or the hegemony of the Prussian Junkers, throughout the West, old-style public administration was put into place in an attempt to 'right a wrong'. Its replacement has already led to concerns that there will be an increase in 'malversation' and corruption (Hood, 1990; Doig, 1995; Smith, 1996).

Core Competencies

With the steady replacement of old-style bureaucracies by NPM, both practitioners and academics have sought to define what are the core functions of government and how they are to be delivered. Once again different states have delivered different answers to these questions. In the US the role of government agencies has been part of the battleground for over twenty years, with each president after Johnson promising to reform and/or reduce the size of the federal bureaucracy, promises replicated by politicians in most of the fifty states of the union. The actual input of senior career officials into the policy process has also wavered, their role and advice being subject to malign neglect under Reagan, selectively ignored under Bush and actively encouraged under Clinton and Gore (Massey 1993; Margetts, Chapter 3, this volume). The power of Congress and the influence of major interest groups has done much to prevent root and branch restructuring and downsizing of the federal bureaucracy; rather a sullen stalemate between the contestants has caused most attempts at reform to founder on the petrified structures of the multiplicity of departments, bureaus and agencies. This is in stark contrast to the fundamental Australian and New Zealand reforms (Domberger and Hall, 1996, pp. 129–47).

The increased marketization of goods and services has impacted upon both the private and the public sectors. Dunleavy (Chapter 2, this volume) provides a sophisticated analysis of its impact upon the role and power of governments to set their own agenda and carry out their functions. Marketization accompanies agencification and is an integral part of NPM, it is also probably irreversible in the short term. If a large government department, such as the tax gathering agency, outsourced its information technology (IT) functions it would take the life of a Parliament to reconstruct the in-house ability to carry out those functions (Margetts, Chapter 3, this volume).

The drive to marketize comes from the search for greater efficiencies (in the public sector) and increased profit. There are several important aspects, but two of the more noticeable are:

1. the shift of certain activities, such as IT, cleaning, accountancy and other professional services, to outside specialist providers which are often branches of large multinational corporations;
2. the shift of manufacturing labour intensive activities to cheap labour economies in the Third World, or modernizing Asian economies unencumbered by Western-style employment practices and legislation.

Both these aspects have been heavily criticized in Europe and the US across the political spectrum, indeed the nationalist right has often seemed more vocal than the left-leaning labour movement with regard to the loss of manufacturing output overseas; witness the campaign of Republican candidate Buchanan in the 1996 American presidential primaries, or the criticism of Sir James Goldsmith in Europe (1995).

The criticism falls under several headings:

- the loss of domestic provision represents a strategic problem of sovereignty for the state, the power to control issues of national importance is compromised (Tolchin, 1996);
- the ability of democratically elected government to act rapidly and flexibly to unforeseen crises is compromised;
- there is a loss of expertise, even competence at the centre, which transfers to the producer power over the provision of goods and services. With this loss government may even lose the ability to be an intelligent customer and will have to resurrect complex contractual arrangements with outside independent consultants to set and enforce contracts, something which in itself may not be possible due to the often monopolistic position of producers and the demands of commercial confidentiality;
- there is a loss of legitimacy for the state. If the government is seen to be little more than a letting agent to profit-seeking private companies, the symbolic functions it has to perform, such as being seen to behave in the national interest, are undermined;
- there is a loss of equity and open justice. Private sector providers will not deliver services to marginal groups, or geographical areas, without substantial state subsidies; if these monies are not forthcoming, the subsequent pruning of services will result in hardship at the margins which further undermines the concept of *national* provision and thereby also further undermines the universal legitimacy of the state and support for it;
- the logical stage to follow this is a general immiseration of the public sphere and a loss of community values and standards as individuals seek to make private provision for those aspects of life from which they perceive the state to be withdrawing.

For ideological liberals the need to reduce the role and size of the state continues, for the most part, to dictate a continuation of this process. Their list of core functions for the role of the state is, therefore, often that of the old *laissez-faire* nightwatchman state. Although the precise nature of what the minimalist state would look like in the twenty-first century is hard to predict, suffice to suggest, it would not look like the old English nightwatchman state of the eighteenth century. For others the core activities are often more numerous.

Like NPM itself, outsourcing is a product of fashion, a fashion moreover which increasingly large sections of private industry are moving away from, especially with regard to the contracting out of IT activities (Alexander and Young, 1996, pp. 116–17). Whereas in the 1980s the fad for delayering and simplifying led to the disaggregating of most company activities, with those deemed non-essential, or non-core activities, being contracted out, recent years have seen an increasingly wide definition of what constitutes core activities. For private corporations, Alexander and Young argue there are at least four meanings of core activities:

1. activities traditionally performed internally with long-standing precedent;
2. activities critical to business performance;
3. activities creating current or potential competitive advantage;
4. activities that will drive the future growth, innovation or rejuvenation of the enterprise (1996, p. 117).

With the exception of the third definition, much of this list is applicable to the public sector, although the boundaries involved around which activities are to be 'ring-fenced' and which are to be hived-out are unclear.

It should be obvious, therefore, that there is no universally acceptable definition of what constitutes the core activities of the state, or even of central government departments (Massey, 1995c). Attempts at providing trait-like lists of activities and functions are often contradictory and are always subject to furious debate and denial (ibid.). Each definition is produced by a model of the state and that in turn is dependent upon one of the four broad social science paradigms identified by Guba. That is, in searching for a definition of core functions academics must confront the *a priori* beliefs of those involved in setting the definition or in agreeing to it.

In any ideologically pluralist setting, therefore, there can be no agreed definition as it is the boundaries and functions of the state that provide the meat and drink of much Western political discourse and conflict. Any definition must be placed within its paradigmatic context and that makes it fair game for those who are themselves located within a different set of values and beliefs. The global post-bureaucratic reform paradigm, therefore, is but one among many. If it is replacing an older paradigm it will remain in conflict with its rivals and will in turn be destabilized and replaced by them or other paradigms. These alternatives include old-fashioned nationalism, as well as more radical options. All (with the exception of the more bizarre anarchistic and syndicalistic models) recognize a role for the state with greater core activities to be carried out by state agencies.

CONCLUSION

There has been a sixty-fold increase in world trade since 1950 (Vogel, 1995, p. 11). The liberalization of trade and the unending search for markets and profits has driven an economic revolution which has impacted upon the political structures of the world, through the establishment of supranational institutions like those of the EU (see Goldsmith, Chapter 4, this volume) and the drive for political reforms to cope with the effect of multinational companies upon national economies. These in turn, along with a string of new liberalizing treaties and trade blocs, such as the General Agreement on Tariffs and Trade (GATT), the North American Free Trade Agreement (NAFTA), the European Union (EU) and the European Free Trade Agreement (EFTA), have further aided the development of the modern global economy.

Yet as Moran and Prosser argue in their study of privatization and regulatory change in Europe, the national context of policy making continues to take precedence over supranational and international settings for several reasons. These include:

- the contingency of history and the resurgence of national sentiment, any attempt to explain marketization 'that ignored the nationalist context would be seriously incomplete';
- the starting point from which each state approaches the restructuring of its economy and its administrative system is unique (1994, pp. 145–6).

Even in an apparently federalizing polity such as the EU the national barriers to trade thrown up by disparate food and hygiene regulations and the impossibility of obtaining a comprehensive environmental policy illustrate the continuing importance of national government (Vogel, 1995, chs 2–3). It is all the more evident when the obvious democratic deficit of the EU's supranational institutions is observed (Goldsmith, Chapter 4, this volume).

The constitutional lacuna in terms of clear, direct lines of accountability caused by the agencification and marketization of government is one that urgently needs to be addressed by national governments. The loss of control over key tools of policy implementation and their usurpation by profit-driven multinational corporations is a threat to the legitimacy of the state and seriously impedes its ability to carry out its democratic mandate. This is a problem in countries throughout the West. To question the marketization of the state is not to pen a mawkish madrigal to some outdated version of the nation state, it is to press the timeless demand for those who have power to account for themselves. If there remains an inalienable core role for the state, it is to protect the citizenry from the venal depredations of those who would prey upon society. It is for that that we have government; indeed, the wisdom of the American Founding Fathers was rooted in the knowledge that if men were angels there would be no need for government. As the state pares down its menu of direct provision, in a global age of rootless multinationals vying to absorb the profitable fodder of tax-funded services, good, effective and accountable government is essential.

NOTES

1. See Hughes, 1994, for a discussion regarding the nomenclature of *public administration versus public management* and *new public management*.
2. See the chapter in this volume by Grant Jordan for a magisterial rebuke of the work of Osborne and Gaebler; also Overman and Boyd (1994) and Hood (1995).

2 The Globalization of Public Services Production: Can Government be 'Best in World'?

Patrick Dunleavy

> 'I know it upsets many people even to contemplate the possibility that we are caught up in social processes not under the control of any human agency.' (Herbert Kaufman, 1978, p. 24)

In the last two decades public administration has had a very poor record of looking forward and correctly anticipating trends and future developments of central relevance to the subject. When Ostrom warned of the 'intellectual crisis in American public administration' and argued for a series of public choice-influenced new approaches, there was little response. Instead, for the next decade and a half the discipline's textbooks and the writings of political scientists lagged further and further behind the wave of practice, less so in America but extremely sharply in Britain where the changes in public sector administration have been so rapid (Elcock, 1991). To take a current UK example, there has been a major erosion of multi-issue local public administration (municipalities and district health authorities) by micro-local agencies in Britain over the last nine years. However, there is as yet no useful description of these agencies, still less a theoretical rationale for introducing them (which is related to Buchanan's theory of clubs, and to the weakness of 'Tiebout forces' given the UK's heavily modernized local government structures and dominant non-local forms of municipal financing).

This pattern of anachronistic public administration approaches, lagging far behind the development of current practice, is likely to change somewhat in future as the current wave of 'new public management' (NPM) reforms stabilizes, and as many of its internal difficulties emerge (Dunleavy and Hood, 1994). Public administration as a discipline has now internalized many NPM ideas and is slowly catching up with new realities by rebuilding a management-orientated orthodoxy to replace the lost certainties of the 1960s and 1970s.

This chapter, however, reflects a conviction that a new and even more fundamental source of disjuncture between academic ideas and administrative practice is opening up unnoticed beneath our feet – the decoupling of public services production from a single-country context. Although privatization and contractorization have progressively created 'markets' of various kinds in public administration over the last fifteen years, the involvement of private

16

corporations has overwhelmingly been organized on a single-country basis. Most political scientists and public administration writers currently seem to believe that the idiosyncracies of national political systems constitute irremovable barriers to the development of broader transnational corporations dominating public services production. In this chapter I argue that the developments of the last decade strongly suggest that these barriers will not prove permanently substantial.

To establish this point I focus on three problematic terms. By 'globalization' I mean the substantial internationalization or regionalization of an activity previously handled in a single-country context. By 'public services' I mean collective consumption provision – those aspects of health, education, social services, transport, housing, infrastructure services, environmental improvement and urban planning organized or subsidized by government; social insurance provision (governmentally-organized unemployment pay, pensions, sickness compensation, and so on); and public administration. By 'production' I mean the direct organization of task implementations or of service provision to take place, rather than policy decisions about what is to be provided or what tasks should be undertaken, all of which form part of the 'purchasing' role (see below).

The argument that the direct implementation of tasks in the public services may cease to be organized in a single-country way, and come to be organized by private corporations operating on a much wider scale, has three sections. First I review the existing impact of NPM on public services production. The second section examines contemporary developments in technology, in private sector organizations, and in broader social structures which create pressures for 'markets' once opened up to enlarge in scale. The third section considers how the impacts of existing public sector shifts and of wider technological and social pressures for change may cumulate in future developments with strong implications for the role of nation states.

NPM AND CHANGES IN PUBLIC SERVICES PRODUCTION

New public management is the domesticated, depoliticized version of 'New Right' or 'market liberal' policy analysis, made somewhat more technical, consensual and generic. The hallmark of the approach is a blend of policy and administrative solutions stressing disaggregation, competition and incentivization. I first review these three main elements and then look at variations in the implementation of NPM.

Disaggregation

New public management is strongly opposed to traditional line hierarchies, large machine bureaucracies, and the functionally organized agencies which predominated from the 1950s to the late 1970s. Instead it emphasizes the chunking-up of public service organizations, creating far more deconcentrated or decentralized patterns. This change is the public sector equivalent of the earlier shift amongst large private corporations from unitary (U-form) patterns of organization to multi-firm (M-form) configurations (Williamson, 1975). Both trends have resulted in smaller, more coherently directed, more single-focused and more fragmented forms of organization. Disaggregation components include:

- *Corporatization and strong organizational leadership.* These goals are achieved by separating out discrete blocks of activity so that they can be separately developed, and accorded a far higher degree of management attention than would be feasible where they are small components of a much larger organization. Concentrating leadership in a single chief executive (by downgrading previously professional or collegial forms of organizational direction) is a common sub-theme of corporatization.

- *The growth of quasi-governmental agencies (QGAs).* Discrete agencies are set up, akin to product-focused firms, separating out specific tasks from multi-issue central government departments (or state/regional governments in federal systems). In strong NPM countries an 'explosion' of QGAs has been a corollary of the corporatization drive.

- *The creation of micro-local agencies (MLAs).* The analogous process at local or municipal level takes responsibility for local services production away from multi-issue municipalities (and health authorities in the UK) single-facility or sub-local, single-function agencies.

- *'Hiving-in' at central government level,* as in the Next Steps programme carries through a similar logic by setting up executive agencies within a loosened civil service framework, to take over discrete blocks of work previously carried out by central government departments.

- *The creation of independent institutions* is a subtly different process. Whereas QGAs, MLAs and executive agencies remain subject to direction by higher tier political institutions (central government ministers in the UK), arguments for independent institutions stress the need to insulate some tasks or activities more completely from political interventions. All examples of corporatization implicitly constrain top decision makers' scope of action, by creating new inter-organizational boundaries which multiply clearance points and circumscribe the scope for direct instruction (Pressman and Wildavsky, 1974). However, top-tier political decision makers commonly dispose of powerful financial, regulatory, policy system, and professional levers over corporatized bodies. With independent institutions these less visible forms of leverage are also screened out, and a potential for bargained or even adversarial processes is built in.

- *Decoupling linked policy systems* is a necessary step in corporatization changes, and usually involves dismantling planning-based systems of co-ordination. Instead more discrete sub-systems are constituted, with interactions handled at a distance, often in contractual or quasi-contractual form, or by the use of formula-based funding schemas (often associated with consumer-tagged financing).
- *'Chunking-up' privatized industries* so as to create multiple producer roles (as well as separating out regulatory roles from producer roles) is another form of disaggregation strategy. It responds to the profound inadequacies of early model privatizations, such as those in the UK which created integrated private sector monopolies in the gas and telephone industries. Simple forms of chunking include separating out large companies into regional units, or more complex efforts to make organizational forms follow role boundaries, as in the UK railway privatization arrangements.
- *'Competition by comparison'* denotes pseudo-competition where the relative performance of chunked-up private industries or corporatized agencies is monitored, and some penalty attaches to laggards. Thus privatized companies in the same industry may strive to be efficient in order to attract capital finance, or good stock market ratings, or more favourable treatment from regulators. Corporatized agencies may want to attract better funding from top-tier decision makers, or to recruit more clients carrying with them tagged finance.
- *Performance measurement* is a generalized NPM strategy, reflecting a long-run development of output measurement, output budgeting, and attributing costs to outputs.
- *League tables* entail extending performance indicators to produce simplified aggregate measures of performance, which can then inform consumers or a wider public of the comparative efficiency or success ratings of different providers.
- *A push towards limited deprofessionalization* follows from numerous pressures already listed – efforts to create strong or corporate leadership, displacing collegial forms of organizational guidance; the substitution of publicized performance indicators and consumers' decisions for

professional evaluations and judgement of success; and the erosion of professional planning by contractual relationships.

Competition

These strategies have in common an effort to remove monopoly suppliers, to establish multiple competing sources of supply or at the least to show the 'contestability' of blocks of work, and thus to create a potential for future competition if a currently dominant supplier exploits their position or fails to maintain efficient technologies or working practices:

- *Splitting up purchasers and providers* means separating out the planning and specification of services to be provided and their financing (the purchasing role), from the direct organization of tasks (the provider role). The rationale here is that even if the purchasing role remains an inherently public sector function, competition between multiple providers can be set in train.
- *Compulsory competitive tendering (CCT) or 'market testing'* then enforces a regime where private firms (and sometimes not-for-profits, mixed bodies or voluntary associations) can always bid against in-house public sector teams, or against a previously successful private contractor, as contracts for service provision periodically come up for renewal.
- *Government-to-government contracting and intragovernmental contracting* extends the logic of multiple providers into areas where for various reasons the retention of service provision within a fully public sector environment is required.
- *Consumer-tagged financing* moves away from assigning budgets directly to 'provider' organizations or facilities, instead linking funding with clients or consumers. This step opens up the possibility of consumers making choices for themselves between competing provider organizations, by 'exiting' from those with declining quality of services and switching to more successful outlets. It also means that more popular or successful organizations or facilities gain larger budgets than less popular ones. Budget size is now directly linked with the scale of activities.
- *Vouchers* take consumer-tagged financing and exit options to a limit by providing clients with a cash equivalent which they can exchange for services in a wider range of outlets, which might be public sector bodies, quasi-governmental agencies or regulated private sector organizations.

- *User control* expands consumers' capabilities beyond 'exit' options to include also 'voice' exercised via complaints, elections, lobbying, protests, and so on in some micro-local agencies (schools, housing estates). Usually in Britain user control has displaced previous patterns of indirect 'community' control, via municipal elections and councillors in local services for example. At a limit, user control may imply single-facility organizations 'opting out' of integrated public service organizations. (The converse does not follow here: many 'opted out' bodies are management controlled and not user controlled.) However, in Scandinavia user control has more often supplemented electoral influences, and been used as a finer-grain system of accountability within integrated public service organizations.

- *Public/private sector polarization and the opening up of new lines of sectoral cleavages* has been used to stimulate 'competition' in the UK, mainly because of the close links of the Conservative Party with 'private' sector social locations and of Labour with public sector locations (Dunleavy, 1989a). Sectoral polarization is a useful macro-strategy because people can be 'bounced' into changing sectors by adjustments in their relative subsidization (as in UK council house sales, or the funding of 'grant maintained' schools compared with local authority schools) (Dunleavy, 1986b). Where sectoral competition is linked with modal consumption choices (for example, private car use versus public mass transit), competition is further intensified.

- *Product market liberalization and deregulation* have become important stimulants for competition, with governments attempting to reintroduce 'entrepreneurial' flair and lower-cost forms of organization into previously stagnant service industries, especially those supported by substantial public subsidies, such as urban bus services (Gomez-Banez and Meyer, 1993).

Incentivization

NPM strongly promotes the use of quasi-pecuniary motivations at an individual level in the public services, or revenue maximization incentives at an organizational level, to supplement or to replace a previous 'public service' ethic focused on professional or organizational/bureaucratic motivations. These 'new' forms of incentives are said to foster greater entrepreneurialism, and closer attention to cost savings and organizational efficiency:

- *The privatization of asset ownership* has been important in applying NPM to government enterprises, and increasingly to 'mainstream' government administration. In both cases the shift reflects a belief that private sector firms are inherently more efficient or dynamic than public sector equivalents – a proposition usually advanced for ideological reasons, and immensely difficult to establish empirically (net of numerous conflicting influences).

- *Respecification of property rights* is a more theoretically based but equivalent component, reflecting a conviction that there must be some optimal configuration of property rights which could minimize problems of conflicting interests or externalities. A key proposition is that vesting an inclusive property right in one (private) actor may produce a better pursuit of an overall social interest than splitting up ownership (Barzell, 1989).

- *'Light touch' regulation* combines an effort to compel efficiency improvements on privatized industries (by specifying price increases less than inflation) with an effort to make regulators independent institutions. 'Regulatory capture' is supposed to be fended off by keeping an arm's-length relationship between regulator and industry (and perhaps also by choosing as regulators economists versed in capture theory).

- *Capital market involvement* broadens incentives acting on public service organizations by partially or wholly substituting private sector financing modes. Investor involvement is expected to increase pressures on managers for cost savings (for example, in planning and undertaking construction work), or in estimating levels of 'market demand' for services.

- *Unifying rates of return and discounting criteria* is achieved by removing previously available public sector finance regimes, especially lower rate of return criteria for funding investments stemming from public sector bodies' reduced risks or exemptions from taxes. Also targeted for change are public sector discounting rates for capital projects alleged to be overly generous to long-term benefits and to underestimate the costs of capital finance.

- *Introducing private financing arrangements* takes this process a stage further by organizationally involving companies in the building, project management and financing of individual public sector investments, an especially innovative departure in relation to 'mainstream' public administration projects. Its rationale turns heavily on the proposition that transferring risk to the private sector will produce superior risk management (especially cost escalation of capital projects) than previous arrangements, gains sufficient to offset the 'paying on credit card' aspect of private finance and leaseback schemes.

- *The development of charging technologies* has emerged as a key NPM innovation in the 1990s, largely due to physical control technology enhancements made possible by better information technology. Examples include the computer coding of electricity packets, thereby allowing competing suppliers to use a common electricity grid and supply network to market energy directly to individual consumers; or the introduction of electronic forms of road pricing, dramatically expanding the scope for private sector provision or maintenance of roads. The shift in charging technologies goes along with the general NPM emphasis on financial viability. It completes the process of displacing cost/benefit analysis and welfare economics criteria from the central position in policy analysis which they held in the 1970s.

- *Valuing and managing the whole public sector equity* entails an extension of NPM so far actually implemented on a large scale only in New Zealand. To run government agencies on lines more directly analogous to private corporations (using 'generally accepted accounting conventions'), public sector managers need to be able to value their organization's total equity, and to have policies to manage its depreciation. The introduction of accrual accounting methods is the basic innovation here.

- *Anti-rent-seeking policies* are a corollary of the expansion of pecuniary incentives. They aim to identify areas where remuneration and outputs are inadequately linked, on the assumption that there is a near-universal tendency for people to try and acquire unearned rents.

- *Deprivileging professions and public sector workers* has been the leading anti-rent-seeking policy associated with NPM, especially in the UK. The strategy focuses on projecting previously 'sheltered' pay formulae, employment relations, pension provisions, and so on, into more 'flexible', private sector forms which remunerate employees more directly in relation to local conditions and market scarcities.

- *Increased pay differentiation*, meaning greatly increased levels of pay inequalities, has followed from the replacement of national pay negotiations by regional or local deals, and by a general tendency for NPM arrangements to depress the pay of the least skilled workers and greatly enhance that of top managers (Hood and Peters, 1994).

- *Performance-related pay* is an extension of the drive against rent seeking, and the introduction of performance indicators. The main problem is the small proportion of pay which is normally performance related. This component is also associated with the introduction of quasi-contractual methods of inter-organizational guidance, and the strategy of building up leadership roles in agencies.

- *Mandatory 'efficiency dividends'* build into public budgeting structures an expectation that public service efficiency will progressively improve. In place of previous assumptions of constant costs, or real-terms inflation, efficiency dividends substitute year-on-year decrements justified by the idea that government organizations will show continuous productivity improvements, just as private firms must do.

Variations in the Take-up of NPM

The scope and scale of NPM changes is impressive, and their cumulative effect in accentuating a drift towards privatized production of public services is enormous. Especially in 'advanced' countries such as Britain and New Zealand (at least in the 1980s) the transformation of public service systems has been dramatic, and the change of cultures even more so. Zifcak records a Treasury under-secretary minuting his colleagues in 1982: 'In my more extravagant/romantic moments I think of us as carrying the torch for change, but modestly, as befits the immensity of the task' (Zifcak, 1994, p. 1). By contrast, in 1993 a key Cabinet Office official complained at a private London School of Economics (LSE) seminar that it was completely anachronistic to see the higher civil service as a bastion against change, given their proven willingness to devise and implement radical reforms of public sector organization. Quite the contrary was true: 'We believe in "permanent revolution"', he said.

Yet it is important to point out some ways in which the purely analytic summing up of NPM changes given above may be misleading. In the first place the characterization of NPM tends towards an 'ideal type'. Not all the changes itemized above are present in all countries or pursued as a coherent strategy even when many of them occur together. Although new public management as a whole is still an ideologically dominant wave in Organization for Economic Co-operation and Development (OECD) countries, there are sharply varying levels of implementation across countries:

- In Britain the third-term Thatcher government inaugurated an across-the-board frenzy of administrative reform on purchaser/provider lines, which was carried forward under Major's 'reform without purpose' regime. The strong faith of senior Cabinet Office and Treasury officials in radical management changes has begun to ebb somewhat in the face of disappointing efficiency results, soaring overhead costs, evidence that the cartelization of providers is impairing competition, the return of large-scale public sector sleaze in corporatized bodies, and rising public dislike of reduced democratic accountability. But the private finance initiative (PFI), contractorization of central government operations, and downsizing of the civil service because of computerization and delayering remain important trends.

The impact of NPM on the constitutional and political equilibrium in Britain has been profound. The central state has virtually *become* a local government in its obsessive pursuit of an administrative reform agenda, in the process disintegrating all sub-national centres of political power. Little wonder then that the UK has been and remains a world leader in contracting out public services production.

- In New Zealand public sector management was radically recast by governments in the 1980s and early 1990s, thanks to a unicameral Westminster system and a conversion by the Labour party to NPM ideas. But in 1992–3 the NPM wave was halted by a strong public backlash. The 1993 election produced effectively a minority government, a further diversification of the party system, and victory for electoral reformers in a constitutional referendum (Mulgan, 1989; Vowles, 1994).

- In Australia the Labour government successfully domesticated NPM in the form of the Financial Management Improvement Programme (FMIP), which compares favourably in its successful implementation with Whitehall's largely defunct FMI (Zifcak, 1994). Australian forms of 'humanized' NPM powerfully influenced Osborne and Gaebler, and via them the Clinton–Gore proposals for reform.

- In the US public management practices were gridlocked under Reagan and Bush, with only minor improvements in federal government financial management practices over twelve years (Massey, 1993). However, the advent of undivided government with Democratic control of the executive and legislature, together with the consensual National Performance Review (NPR) opened up some potential for substantial changes in federal administration, which the NPR's 'humanistic' elements seemed to encourage (Margetts, 1994; Peters, 1994). In the event, the Republican landslide in the 1994 Congressional elections recreated divided government and shifted progress into a more ideological right-wing tilt, with Congress simply downsizing the bureaucracy, and the administration responding with an 'NPR2' focusing on privatization and further contractorization.

- In Scandinavia NPM's influence has been limited to the privatization of some service delivery in local and central government. However, there are fairly distinctive (perhaps 'Nordic NPM') elements in these changes, such as the combination of competitive tendering in municipal services with an emphasis on decentralization at neighbourhood level within democratic municipal structures.

- In Germany there has been little adoption of NPM to date, due to constitutional constraints, the lack of party consensus, and a strong public service orientation towards legalistic forms of policy analysis and management. The severe recession in the early 1990s, plus strong efforts by the Social Democratic Party (SPD) to increase its electoral standing by embracing a humanized form of NPM, may trigger a break-up of the previous logjam. Moves towards corporatization of public utility enterprises have been made, following experience of privatizing former government enterprises in the new eastern *Lander*.
- Japan has been virtually immune to NPM ideas at the central ministry level. Some public enterprises (railways and telecoms) were privatized in the 1980s. In the 1990s the main reform efforts have concentrated on changing Japan's electoral law (to a proportional representation system) and combating political corruption. The advent of coalition governments in place of single-party (Liberal Democratic Party) dominance may indicate a potential for loosening up 'feudal' civil service operations, but only over the long term (see Margetts and Smyth, 1994).
- Italy has been another country where public bureaucracy changes generally hung fire for much of the 1980s. The installation of new election laws at local government level (creating a reinforced majority for the winning mayor's list on each council) and at national level (creating a majority for new right-wing parties in 1994), may herald a drive for greater efficiency, while anti-corruption feeling sustains a push for greater financial accountability and productivity. Privatization may appeal as a means of pursuing multiple objectives simultaneously. But the inertial weight of conventional bureaucracy and clientelism may be hard to shake.

The overall impact of variations in NPM will be to fragment at least for the immediate future the adoption of the full NPM agenda, slowing down the development of a cross-national or generally international market potential in the public services. The linkage between different parts of the NPM project will be obscured, and its similarities to private sector modes of operating will be less visible, for a time.

Second, there is now little doubt that NPM has become a differentiated movement of change, although there is little scholarly agreement yet on the most fruitful ways of considering variations within NPM. One approach argues that the most authentic (that is, right-wing) form of NPM is a minimal purchasing state where the public and private sectors operate in very similar ways, and where there is little distinctive regulation of the public sector. But in practice most systems of organization so far affected by NPM changes have not moved into this configuration. Instead administrative systems have generally moved away from conventional public administration without necessarily coming any closer to the minimal state situation. Some areas of government have become less organizationally differentiated from the private sector, while nonetheless remaining highly regulated spheres of social life – the so-called 'gridlock' governance (Dunleavy and Hood, 1994). Other administrative systems have been deregulated, with overall plans being scrapped or replaced by efforts at creating competition between providers, but with public sector organizations nonetheless remaining very different in their pattern of organization from private sector corporations – a pattern which could be labelled 'headless chicken' governance (Dunleavy and Hood, 1994).

A different way of picturing the various strands of NPM focuses on political hostility to an extended state role, and the stability/fluidity of the scope of government activities (Margetts and Dunleavy, 1994). The core of new public management is technical or consensual NPM, where political hostility is medium and the scope of government activities is fairly stable. Other approaches include 'ideological' or 'New Right' NPM pursued where the scope of government is stable but political hostility is high (for example, the Gingrich-style Republican policy in the US); or 'humanist' NPM pursued by governments basically friendly to state intervention but where the scope of government intervention is in practice quite fluid (as in Australia under Labour governments from 1984 into the 1990s). However, the most important contemporary differentiation in NPM is between the 'residualization' form apparently being practised in the UK with the 'market testing' programme for contracting out civil service tasks, and the 're-engineering' form of NPM indicated by the first wave of Gore's National Performance Review, where until 1994 the focus was on genuinely improving the efficiency of government by careful redesign of tasks and procedures, rather than on simply cutting back government (Hammer and Champy, 1993; NPR, 1993).

A final important point about NPM is that there is currently little or no basis for arguing that NPM strategies objectively increase the effectiveness of public sector organizations. There is scant evidence that the adoption of NPM triggers or facilitates economic success. On the other hand, there is a suggestive link between the onset of economic stringency and a shift by governments towards adopting NPM strategies. Since the enthusiasm for NPM has virtually all the characteristics of a 'policy boom', in many instances its adoption may simply be symbolic, the adoption of rituals deemed legitimate by significant elites, whether or not they have any effect (Meyer and Rowan,

1977). Hence NPM proponents have probably overstated the direct ameliorative effects of public sector management reforms in improving social problem solving. And they have neglected completely or underestimated two indirect effects:

- the negative impacts of some NPM changes in reducing the level of citizens' autonomous capacity to solve their problems, a capacity which in most cases makes a critical contribution to social problem-solving; and
- the impacts of many NPM strategies in increasing the level of problem complexity. For example, disaggregation increases the number of clearance points, competition increases residualization trends, and incentivization often reduces trust and increases instrumental behaviour in public sector organizations. Since problem complexity is also a key negative influence on social problem solving, boosting it reduces welfare and offsets the positive direct impacts claimed for NPM strategies.

Because these effects are indirect, however, it is perfectly feasible for the NPM movement to continue or intensify for many years before triggering reconsideration or a public opinion backlash (such as that in New Zealand, or the 'post-privatization blues' in the UK).

WHY GLOBALIZATION OF PUBLIC SERVICE PRODUCTION IS LIKELY

If NPM changes contribute powerfully to pressures for privatization, in themselves they say nothing about the scale on which public service production is organized. Where NPM policies have been vigorously implemented, it is widely assumed that the separation of purchasers from providers and the chunking-up of previous functionally integrated organizations may produce a very diversified pattern of producer organization. Public services production could end up being carried out by a huge and motley array of mostly small and unconsolidated organizations, such as small-to-medium private sector firms, not-for-profit organizations, contractorized governmental units, private practice professionals, independent institutions, quasi-governmental agencies, managerial MLAs, user-controlled MLAs, voluntary associations or even interest groups. Pluralist political science has already highlighted policy communities, policy networks and 'advocacy coalitions' as the key loci of much effective policy change in contemporary liberal democratic societies

(Marsh and Rhodes, 1992; Sabatier and Jenkins-Smith, 1993; Dowding, 1994; Mills and Saward, 1994). If the benign picture of NPM leading to increasingly diversified producers of public services is realized, then public policy would inevitably come to be made in a new multi-organizational, contractualized form of policy communities and networks. Public/private sector boundaries would be blurred at the same time as purchaser/provider distinctions were formally sharpened. In practice we might expect 'corporatist' intermediation processes to create a progressively more integrated consensus in stable NPM systems, especially where changes of providing organizations rarely occur. Consumer/producer distinctions would also be sharpened, except where services are provided in user-controlled MLAs or voluntary organizations.

My purpose in this section, however, is to consider whether other influences are pushing towards the creation of a very different future – one in which public service production is increasingly carried out in quasi-monopolistic or oligopolistic 'markets', by large and specialized corporations organized on transnational lines – which would determine what is feasible or not, what policy alternatives are available, what technologies are employed, and what treatments are attempted in the public services. I first review a number of market pressures for this form of globalization, and, second, the forces internal to the state apparatus pushing in the same direction.

Market Pressures for Globalization

There are five principal 'market' pressures for the globalization of private services production, all of which are likely to have important corollaries or implications for public services production: the contemporary growth of services, changes in technology, new forms of commercial and industrial organization by firms, the development of radical outsourcing, and changes in commodification processes.

Services growth represents an important change in contemporary societies, as a range of authors has extravagantly claimed over the years (Rostow, 1960; Bell, 1974). Compared with goods instantiated in physical products, services are famously hard to define. Weber defined goods as 'non-human objects which are the potential source of utilities of whatever sort', and services as 'utilities derived from a human source, so far as this source consists in active conduct' (Weber, 1947, p. 151). This residual form of definition still persists, as in *The Economist*'s dictum that services are 'anything sold in trade that could not be dropped on your foot' (qouted in Quinn, 1992, p. 6).

The black box character of services has produced very important misconceptions in previous authors who hailed a 'services revolution' and the coming of a 'post-industrial society', when there is much evidence that services growth reflects in part a changing organizational division of labour in the production and marketing of *goods*, changes which disguise the long-run decline of previously important services (such as domestic service) and their displacement by consumer durables and 'do-it-yourself' equipment (Gershuny, 1978). This sorry record of misdiagnosis has not stopped new generations of services enthusiasts talking in cornucopianist terms of 'an endless horizon' of economic development and the 'perpetual growth opportunities' in prospect, without reference to any difficulties from satiation, under-consumption/over-production crises, or environmental and resource limits:

> The capacity of services to create value is limited only by the capacity of human imaginations to think up more important things to do with their time as intermediate customers or final customers – and the imaginations of others to think up better ways to serve their customers' health, financial, communications, transportation, entertainment, security, distribution, storage, lodging, gastronomic, education, design, information, comfort, cultural, environmental, public service and specialized knowledge needs. (Quinn, 1992, p. 436)

Behind the froth, however, there lies a kernel of important possibilities for changes in the organization of social tasks. Services growth focusing on new products (many of which, like financial futures and complex forms of asset holding, are really pseudo-products or even virtual reality 'products'), or new techniques or processes (such as enormously speeded-up financial trading), can have real implications. The cumulative impacts in restructuring advanced industrial economies have become fundamental especially in leading-edge corporations. Old stereotypes of services as low productivity, low investment, labour-intensive and non-export industries have been decisively challenged by innovations in service markets and the scale and pace of investment in service capital (Quinn, 1992, pp. 339–64).

Technological changes have provided a strong underpinning for these developments in two ways. First, there has been a dramatic extension of the traditional 'productivist' emphasis of industrial organization on ever-finer task specification, routinization of operations, speeding-up and automation of processes, and attribution of costs. Traditionally the modern capitalist drive towards intensive micro-management, continuous cost reduction, and re-engineering to avoid problems has been applied to physical production and design issues. It is now adressed equally intensively to all aspects of firms' activities – support activities, services elements, R&D and innovation, and even top-level decision making – penetrating areas previously seen as most intangible or judgemental. Technological change has been very linked with product redesign and repackaging. The disaggregation emphasis of NPM has been operating far longer in private industry, fuelling major increases in management attention to non-production areas, and stimulating huge investments and large-scale capital intensification, despite the chronic difficulties of tracking improvements into value-change or showing a bottom-line positive effect on profits.

Second, extremely rapid changes in information technology (IT) areas, and dramatic cheapening and controllability of processing power, have produced an 'informatization' transformation of leading-edge industrial and commercial organizations. The first wave of IT changes essentially automated pre-existing modes of organization, but later waves have progressively affected organization's tasks, missions, products, and fundamental ways of operating. The controllability and portability of information, and its increasing cumulation on an altogether vaster and more detailed scale than previously possible, has accentuated the value of information and made feasible both wholly new products, and more targeted ways of implementing or marketing pre-existing goods and services (Quinn, 1992, ch. 13; cf. Strassmann, 1990).

Information technology has increasingly become a constitutive element of the distinctively modern form of Weber's rationalization processes. Its impacts on organizational culture (and hence on most modern organization theory) has been limited, however, by the operation of displacement effects. Activities which are automated no longer command the same human actor involvement or interest that they previously did, so that the locus of 'problems' in the organization (that is, aspects demanding management attention and correctable by improved decision making) shifts elsewhere. Hence the impact of technological change in transforming organizations is often underestimated by those most affected because of countervailing adjustments in their internal organizational cultures. But with critically important service procedures often already hard-wired into information systems, and with Simon's supposedly immutable cognitive limits on individuals' and organizations' capacities to process information pushed back further each year, the current decade will certainly see a huge increase in mass standardized services fuelled principally by IT developments.

New forms of organization have been made feasible by these shifts. The 'span of control' concept so central to traditional line hierarchical modes of organizing, especially in unified or functionally integrated organizational configurations, has been rapidly eroded. Modern IT-intensive organizational control systems allow for very large numbers of subordinate units to be handled by a single central core of servicing units, providing information, specialized support, regulation, logistical services and capital – a pattern of so-called 'infinitely flat organization' (Quinn, 1992, pp. 113–20).

A key element here is a strong version of the same disaggregation principle discussed above. The private sector version focuses on developing large organizations with very great market presence by defining 'minimum replicable units' (very often service outlets, such as branches of a chain restaurant like McDonald's, or garages owned by a major oil company like BP), which operate in very tightly specified and exactly similar ways (Quinn, 1992, pp. 103–9). These units are then multiplied and disseminated, establishing a carefully standardized company presence in diverse countries and regions. Such 'cloning' strategies evade many of the problems of 'ever-increasing control' and 'counter-control' which plague hierarchical dealings between traditional top tier and lower tier bureaucracies (Downs, 1967). Instead relationships between branches and the corporate centre are tightly focused and controlled within a contractual, franchising or other rule-governed and highly systematized format, while operational linkages are so far as possible automated and focused down on a few strategic interactions.

Radical outsourcing strategies have had far-reaching effects on services growth and reorganization of corporations by splitting up previously unitary organizational configurations. The approach insists on the primacy of intellectual and knowledge-based developments as the 'core competencies' of corporations. Outsourcing, knowledge-based enterprise, service production and the expansion of information systems hang together as components of a 'new paradigm' of 'intelligent enterprise' (Quinn, 1992, p. 213). Company managements should ask whether they are (or could be) 'best in world' at a given activity they currently pursue. If the answer is no, then the firm should consider outsourcing that activity. By continuing to do something in-house when it is clear that rival firms do it better, the corporation is inherently sacrificing comparative advantage, whether in price, or efficiency or effectiveness terms.

Effective companies are those which focus in depth on those areas where they have and can maintain a significant comparative advantage, which will generally involve identifying skills and intellectual capabilities that can be constantly improved and built upon. If the company is 'best in world' at an activity, then it must be recognized as a core competency of the firm, something to be nourished and shielded, carried on in-house, intensively managed, and protected from all forms of competitive erosion in the future. A small number of strategically necessary activities will also often have to be retained in house without meeting the 'best in world' criterion, because they are so important for protecting the core competencies of the firm from erosion by competitors (Quinn, 1992, pp. 53–5).

Changes in commodification processes lie at the heart of contemporary globalization shifts, which some critics see as the realization of a debased, commercialized form of the Enlightenment ideal of a universal liberating civilization. In its place we have progressively established a kind of 'Macworld' capitalism, where product choices whether for hamburgers or computers are increasingly homogenized and standardized across all countries, and where systems and tastes are alike controlled and developed in a proprietary mode by large corporations – challenged only by the diverse (often repellent) forces of 'jihad', affirming local identities through struggle (Barber, 1991). The scale of markets and competition has decisively escalated in some areas, screening out local solutions and corporations in favour of transnational companies, dominant brands and standardized solutions. Cultural barriers to product acceptance have crumbled even in areas where they once seemed insurmountable. In other cases increased preference-pooling has preserved or even enlarged the diversity of choices open to consumers in any one country, at the same time routinizing the exotic so that it becomes familiar (often in subtly adapted forms). The result is that single-market choices expand, but the overall range of choices across different countries' markets may reduce. Cross-national learning mechanisms also seem undeniably to have increased, with shortened diffusion of innovation times. Although some dimensions of 'globalization' arguments are acutely problematic – for example, the argument that economic or political 'interdependence' has increased – these changes are substantial.

For example, suppose in the late 1940s one had been compiling a list of industries where significant globalization would occur over the next half century, then the restaurant industry would surely not have figured anywhere on it. In the 1940s the industry was an exceptionally low-concentration, low capital intensity, non-brand name area. Most firms were very small, with little capital and a craft method of working. Markets were overwhelmingly local, and highly idiosyncratic one from another, with strong culinary and cultural barriers to change. Yet now the fast food corporations such as McDonald's have built up huge businesses by investing in heavily standardized food production and preparation technologies, and intensive marketing of standardized products which are sold in huge numbers in virtually identical form and settings in many different countries. The developments which have already taken place would defy virtually any rational assessment of the prospects for internationalization of the restaurant market fifty years ago.

This example also illustrates a final important aspect of contemporary commodification processes. Large fast-food chains companies compete with numerous smaller, localized providers not just in terms of the food they provide but in terms of *how* customers are served. A key sales point is the speed and character of service, rather than the actual food served – which is in most cases simply routine. Modern commodification processes often focus not on goods themselves, considered as whole bundles or packages instantiated in a physical product, but rather on what Lancaster (1974) terms the 'characteristics' of goods – which can be isolated and highlighted by technological management combined with heavy marketing. Both goods and services have increasingly been disaggregated into their component characteristics, and some features previously seen as unalterable or of minor importance have formed the focus for globally sized corporations' efforts.

The particular contemporary significance of intangible services characteristics has been most evident amongst those corporations supplying basically standardized products and competing heavily in terms of point-of-service discriminators. For example, the 'friendliness' of their staff may be crucial for airlines, hotel chains or fast-food outlets in establishing a market identity (usually in combination with heavy advertising).

State Pressures for Globalization

Within the public sector, there are analogous pressures for globalization, and some key differentiating features. I consider the bureau-shaping incentives acting on bureaucrats and public officials, the potential for radical outsourcing in the public sector, the impacts of government procurement rules, and consequent changes affecting the commodification of public services.

Bureau-shaping incentives have emerged as dominant bureaucratic responses to the end of the post-war growth era in public services employment in the 1980s (Dunleavy, 1991, ch. 8). Rationally self-interested bureaucrats have little stake in maximizing budgets and expanding empires, as older public choice models suggested (Niskanen, 1971). Instead of trying to increase their near-pecuniary utilities (a frustrating task in the public services), senior officials will seek to maximize their work-related utilities, insulating themselves from dependence on a high level of total budget, seeking to reduce exposure to public criticism, to simplify their work tasks, and to concentrate on rewarding and high-status activities (Dunleavy, 1991, ch. 7). All these objectives are best achieved by remodelling their organizations as far as possible to create small, central, elite, staff agencies where senior officials can concentrate their energies. These reshaped central government bureaus then set priorities and move money around to hived-off executive agencies, quasi-governments, private contractors or diversified networks of sub-central agencies. In turn, subordinate agencies will engage in their own forms of bureau shaping, retaining some key strategic decision making or allocational capabilities but often themselves 'load-shedding' production tasks to contractors or voluntary sector bodies. The cumulative result of bureau shaping may then be a chain of 'boutique bureaucracies', down which resources are passed with different agencies creaming off their overhead costs en route.

Both budget-maximizing models in public choice, and everyday stereotypes of bureaucracies as inertially guided, unsteerable organizations, lead us to expect minimal change in response to the contemporary NPM challenge because of bureaucratic resistance, especially by senior officials. By contrast the bureau-shaping model predicts that senior policy makers will over-promote changes such as privatization, corporatization, hiving off and deinstitutionalization, even when they reduce social welfare.

New public management strategies are perfectly consistent with bureau reshaping, and expanding senior managers' utilities. They load costs or potential risks primarily onto agencies' grass-roots workers, middle management (perhaps increasingly in an era of 'expert systems') and agency clients. So the potential for change stems both from corporations' efforts to move into and colonize public service production, *and* from rational bureaucrats and politicians' predisposition to accept rapid bureau reshaping. There is a strong potential for senior bureaucrats to favour reducing the scope of state agencies and capabilities beyond optimal levels if their utilities are thereby maximized. This willingness to embrace change even when it damages the public interest is analogous to the bureau-shaping incentive not to expand into areas involving difficult problems (such as combating the growth of homelessness in advanced industrial countries). Bureau-shaping incentives also work in diametrically opposite ways to, for example, the re-engineering approach to task reorganization (Hammer and Champy, 1993). Bureau shaping pushes officials towards residualizing or outsourcing tasks, paring down their involvement, and renouncing production responsibilities – in the process almost certainly avoiding any committed or creative attempt to reimagine the most effective ways of implementing services.

Radical outsourcing in the public sector entails generalizing the 'best in world' criteria from firms' and corporations' activity to apply also to public service operations. Quinn never considers how his prescriptions might work if transposed to the public sector, but the consequences could be far-reaching. Governments will find it extraordinarily hard to meet the 'best in world' criterion applied to many or most of their service activities. As large corporations progressively develop and refine their capabilities in current or new implementation areas (for example, fields like information systems management, or 'criminal justice services') they will often be able to acquire extra focus in depth, to make large capital investments, and to reap economies of scale by producing standardized service packages across many different localities, regions or countries. Unlike most governmental units, corporations are able to rapidly change their scope of operations by merging, setting up partnership deals, or franchising, so that scale escalation in the corporate economy can rather quickly affect public services production. Major corporations are already emergent in key public service areas, and they will be able to take seriously 'best in world' criteria. In this perspective the prospect of trans-European or transglobal firms becoming major players in defining and developing public services production is by no means remote.

The bureau-shaping model also sheds light on the scope for radical outsourcing inside government. Empirical work in this perspective comparing the central governments of the US, UK, Australia and New Zealand has demonstrated the existence of a number of distinctive agency types (Dunleavy, 1989b, 1992; Dunleavy et al., 1994). The biggest potential for a large-scale shift to contracting lies with delivery agencies, where public officials directly organize implementation of public services. This kind of agency is heavily concentrated in the defence and law and order fields at national government level, both areas where governments have historically maintained fully public operations. However, conceptions of what tasks need to be handled by state employees and what can be hived-off have shifted radically in the last decade and will change further. In defence 'front-line' personnel will remain in large government line agencies, but there is enormous scope for logistical, back-up and research and analysis staffs to be parcelled up into separate agencies, which can be first corporatized and later privatized. In law and order very similar processes apply, with uniformed police employment focusing on front-line staffs while back-up operations are progressively 'civilianized', and contractorization of courts and prisons operations proceeds fast. There are also delivery agencies in other domestic policy areas in all national governments, where the intense restrictions of the defence and law and order fields do not apply. Large national taxing agencies are important too; the scope for contractorization here is similar to delivery agencies, and is well advanced in some areas, such as information system operations. Margetts (1995) clearly documents how the disposal of UK central government's information system management contracts encompassed a tiny group of major global companies, capable of absorbing thousands of transferred civil servants and operating massive computer systems. If we drop down to the state/regional level, or to the level of municipalities and urban policy agencies, the importance of delivery agencies is greater, along with staff sizes – indicating a huge scope for contractorization (Osborne and Gaebler, 1992), albeit in somewhat less oligopolistic markets.

However, at the national government level most public monies already flow through agencies without much direct executant capacity – transfer agencies which shift subsidies to private sector individuals or enterprises, contract agencies which rely on corporations to implement policy, and control agencies which route money to subordinate public sector bodies. The scope for contractorization here is more limited than with delivery agencies, since the levels of public staffing are lower. Nonetheless, large national transfer operations (such as the Social Security Agency in the US or the Benefits Agency in the UK), and the substantial defence contracting agencies, can be further chunked-up and many of their components contractorized. At a limit even the policy development and advice roles at the heart of central government departments might be made the subject of competition, albeit under probably distinctive or more complex contracting arrangements (Boston, 1992).

Government sector procurement rules normally add a strong impetus towards less diversified competition when contractorization does take place. For most of the post-war period it is arguable that national governments in particular have been developing a 'shadow state' based on procurement, where employees of nominally private entities (corporations, universities, research laboratories and so on) work full-time on government contracts, often carrying out tasks indistinguishable from those handled in-house by government employees (Garvey, 1992). In the US, Garvey suggests a rule-of-thumb estimate that for every orthodox federal employee there is at least one 'shadow state' person.

The area of contractorized work is apparently a domain where the imperative acting on public sector agencies does not apply – where pressures for accountability, confidentiality, scrupulous auditing, progressive personnel practices, and sensitivity to political imperatives can be evaded or toned down. Instead as Garvey observes, the shadow state operates on lines seemingly well captured by the new institutional economics, with all qualitative relationships transmuted into contractual specifications and penalties. Yet as the new institutional economics also emphasizes, it is very hard to achieve a complete contract (Williamson, 1985). Governments confront severe *ex ante* problems in fully specifying contract requirements, and *ex post* difficulties of haggling over how things actually turned out.

A key means by which governments have coped with the potential difficulties of spot contracting in markets has been using procurement to encourage industrial concentration. The most common government solution has been for contracts to be awarded to a smallish group of large, oligopolistic contractors, kept in competition to ensure price restraints, but also sufficiently large to internalize 'responsibility' requirements. Bureaus are also concerned about maintaining long-term relations with government. Traditionally the means of fostering industrial concentration via procurement included encouraging negotiated tenders rather than open competition, serial contracting, enlarging the scale of contracts (so as to exclude small suppliers), technological development, and pre-screening of contractors. For more routine purchases many Western governments have now moved back to open competitive contracting, especially for standard components. And periodic attempts are made to counter the obsolescence often built into procurement rules, such as the apocryphal stories of US federal agencies having to fill in a paper train of twenty-three forms before purchasing personal computers (Margetts, 1994).

In more policy-relevant and politically sensitive areas, however, procurement procedures still emphasize significant restraints on competition which principally serve to create oligopolies dominated by large often transnational corporations. Minimum size rules often exclude small firms from tendering, very important in areas such as the contracting out of government computer system operations, where the scale of public sector systems often means that only very large suppliers are credible tenderers. Quality of service constraints on competition have similar effects, especially where a company's size, record and marketing effort provide officials with the best available proxy indicators of its likely 'quality'. And contracting requirements such as equal opportunity policy create thresholds which are easier for large firms to surmount. The European Union's 'transfer of undertakings' (TUPE) regulations make it virtually infeasible for any but the largest companies to take over substantial blocks of government work with associated employees, a favourite mode of contractorization under the UK 'market testing' approach. None of these points necessarily suggest that the push towards oligopolistic relations in procurement is not public interested. There is a huge potential for ruthless private contractors to exploit cases where the social and internal costs of public sector provision diverge (Dunleavy, 1986a), and this tendency can be countered to some degree by pre-selecting or filtering contractors.

Current public sector contracting rules also place a premium on suppliers not deriving super-normal profits from government. These rules offer perverse incentives for high-capability corporations to seek to influence the substantive content of policies in ways favourable for them. In addition to negotiated tenders, serial contracts, and so on, companies essentially search for policy characteristics which can serve as profit surrogates, such as the use of forefront high technology (which encourages proprietorial solutions and screens out competition, while government often subsidizes R&D efforts), gold-plating contracts (which boosts the level of sophistication demanded, and accentuates information impactedness), proprietorial systems development (which locks-in government to unique solutions hard for other contractors to meet), and direct marketing of solutions by corporations to politicians, the mass media and the general public (see below). Asset specificity in government contracting is also high, and will not decrease much despite service automation being generalized across public and private sectors, strengthening companies' incentives to lobby for policy changes favourable to their interests.

The current wave of deregulation in government procurement, such as Clinton's National Performance Review, can be seen as partly countering and partly accentuating previous patterns of development (NPR, 1993). Purges of regulations are needed because fixed, rule-bound procurement regulations tend to decay, constantly lagging behind changes in physical technologies (such as the cheapening of processing power) and behind companies' learned ability to extract rents (unearned profits) from the rules. Devices such as computerized contracting may allow governments to shift back towards spot contracting on markets, rather than oligopolistic contracting or holding huge inventories. But they are likely to only open up competition again for a time, and only then on less complex items – basic PCs, for example, but not 'system integrating' IT contracts. Additionally it is possible that a cycle exists where a deregulation stage is followed by renewed pressure for consolidating procurement with large suppliers if 'sleaze' issues grow.

Commodification processes in the public services have already been changed by new public management techniques. It is now the conventional wisdom that NPM's stress on competition (and pseudo-competition) between providers makes marketing a key tool in public service administrators' armoury. In a diffuse but important way even the advent of diversified quasi-markets, with multiple single-facility suppliers, has begun an important transition towards marketizing the public services. Since such trends are emergent only, it is currently hard to envision their long-term effects.

But we know from a mass of existing research that markets have tremendous significance in shaping social behaviour in general:

> The indirect effect of the market on the way we think is substantial. We assume without thought that goods are exchanged for precise money amounts and not given in the manner of exchange gift economies. We think of goods as individually and not collectively owned and that their usufruct pertains to their individual owners. We accept that we must earn our living in the labour market, that it is shameful to be dependent on kin, that the money in our pockets is exchangeable for commodities, and so forth ... [W]hat we ... think about often (but certainly not always) reflects what we have *learned* from the market. To a large extent the assumptions that we learn are, in fact, *causal theories* about ourselves and the institutions that affect our lives. (Lane, 1991, p. 26)

Marketization trends in the public services are likely to be particularly significant in breaking down historically strong beliefs about the separation of different 'spheres' of social life from each other, some appropriate to market allocations while in others society creates 'blocked exchanges' in order to insulate the allocation of goods from money or power influences (Walzer, 1983).

A number of developments have supplementary effects in the same direction. In modern capitalism there is a strong drift in consumer responses towards private sector point-of-service standards, areas where government enterprises and public service agencies find it very difficult to compete (Lane, 1983, 1986). Marketization gives these generalization and comparison effects an extra spiral, and accentuates a push for the public services to compete increasingly in terms of point-of-service characteristics, especially encouraged by New Right governments. At the same time the personal interaction between government officials and citizens has been progressively reduced by cutbacks in government personnel and reliance on other means of citizens interacting with government, such as mail, phone and, increasingly, electronic communications. The US federal government predicts that 85 per cent of its interactions with citizens will occur via electronic media by the year 2000, and ambitious targets of a similar kind are seen as a key to civil service staff reductions in the UK. This trend may further fix citizens' perceptions on impersonal indicators of government responsiveness and effectiveness.

An inherent consequence of NPM strategies is that citizens will interact increasingly with service providers and not with purchasers. And because providers are more likely to develop up-to-the-minute methods for managing point-of-service issues whereas purchasing bodies will be relatively poor at handling such matters, citizens will see providers in a better light whereas purchasers appear more bureaucratic, out of touch and unresponsive. Who citizens interact with may also come to be even more class structured than it already is. Tendencies for public services to become more exclusively residual or safety net provision will mean that the poor and underprivileged will have most frequent contact with 'mainstream' government agencies (such as welfare bureaucracies). By contrast, middle-income groups may deal overwhelmingly with providers acting on government's behalf, or with mixed public/private provision systems.

All these developments in different ways clear the ground for a transformation of the commodification dynamic in public services so that in future a relatively few large companies are able to put a proprietorial stamp on what is being supplied. If companies can come up with simplified packages, attractive to high- or middle-income groups, and develop some brand distinctiveness, then the stage is set for public service 'products' to first be marketed intensively to intermediate consumers (purchasing agencies), and later (when the market is better established) to final consumers, who can put pressure on intermediate purchasers. In this future, the normal processes of 'commodification' inherent in modern consumer markets would operate between providers and purchasers, with product innovations developed and marketed on lines similar to, say, the modern drugs industry. Consumers' role here might involve exerting pressure on purchasers to buy into one package of services or another, whether based on direct experience or on company advertising. Such a development can give an important boost to the 'circularity' of polyarchies and market systems noted by Lindblom (1977), whereby capitalism creates its own social demand and business occupies a privileged position among all social actors.

IMPACTS ON THE NATION STATE

Up to now the state has been the primary actor in the field of politics and the collective life of society, with a highly distinctive set of defining features. The state could be briefly defined as a set of institutions with a unitary purpose, making collective decisions in a binding way, creating a specialized 'public' sphere, monopolizing the legitimate use of force in a given territory, able to define members and non-members of the society, making strong ideological/ethical claims, commanding a bureaucratic apparatus, financed by taxes and operating via a legal system and a constitution (Duunleavy, 1993). It is worth briefly considering the impacts which large-scale contractorization to large corporations could have on the operations of contemporary states, especially in the context of the development of the European Union and of the internationalization of much previously domestic policy making.

Corporatization and the State

The development of NPM in Britain, New Zealand and possibly Australia has already had observable effects in reducing the distinctiveness of state institutions, a trend which the full NPM agenda promises to push further. The unitary character of nation state institutions is eroded when integrated planning systems give way to quasi-markets and a jungle of QGAs. The dichotomy between formally public and formally private spheres is deeply blurred as contractual relations pyramid upon each other. NPM has also eroded the role of legal systems and constitutional constraints in terms of government operations, for although re-regulation may be seen as inherent in fully specified contracts, the law involved is essentially the civil law of contract.

In many more subtle ways NPM also reduces the distinctiveness of public sector practices, for example, substituting appointment processes for elections, compensating senior public managers with 'prize money' salaries, and linking remuneration not to legal obligations or respect for the public interest or planning for the long-term, but to short-term organizational 'performance'. Finally NPM tends to undermine the importance of most of the conventional arms of government, those activities where previously government was seen as acting uniquely, with a capacity denied to any other social actors. Thus tax raising is displaced by charging, and tax collection could soon be once again hived off to 'tax farmers' on the eighteenth century or even Roman Empire pattern: public administration debt-collecting is already widely handled in this way. Bureaucratic organization and direct implementation capabilities have already changed extensively at the national level under the patterns of 'non-executant' government built up over the post-war period. Similar changes are now under way in Britain's organizationally much larger local government, under the guise of creating 'enabling' local authorities.

Increasingly the special characteristics of government may come to inhere less in physically observable or humanly populated organizations. More and more 'statehood' may come to be constituted by quite small-seeming features of large-scale and socially central information systems, finance raising systems, budget dissemination systems, and rule making systems. The methods by which 'government' systems then interact with the parallel or rival systems of corporations, individuals, voluntary associations and other elements of civil society will also change radically, especially with the growth of electronically mediated communication.

These prospective changes are unlikely to be coolly chosen by decision makers well informed about the future and secure in a well developed conception of what 'statehood' consists in and the steps needed to maintain 'governmentality'. Instead decision makers will make hundreds and thousands of little decisions, with scant regard for long-term consequences. A particular stimulus driving NPM is likely to be a continuing climate of financial stringency in recession-prone governments, and of anti-government feeling in more successful states – the continuing reverberations of the 'fear of bureaucracy' surge in the 1980s which Kaufman (1981) aptly characterized as a 'raging pandemic'. The public services are also passing through an era of extremely rapid evolution of information technology and scarce supply of IT capabilities, with potentially important consequences for government administration (Hood and Margetts, 1993). Restrictions on public sector investment funds have made it very difficult for government agencies to match the strong investment by private corporations in services IT and production methods. Government agencies have shifted from being technological pioneers or leaders (especially in big computer systems) to an increasingly passive role, with the lead in development passing firmly to large IT corporations and consultancies, and indirectly to corporate IT purchasers.

As public service contractorization and commodification processes change in the future, these factors may create a 'coerced exchange' situation for governments. Here policy makers may be forced into outsourcing not because demonstrable social welfare gains will result, but simply because welfare levels will otherwise decrease. The predicted consequence of this combination of forces is over-use of outsourcing, unintended loss of strategic state capacities, outward drift of the ability to specify public service outputs from government, and growth of producer power.

Current NPM thinking identifies government's optimal role, its core distinctive function, as being an 'intelligent consumer' on behalf of citizens, purchasing privately supplied services so as to maximize the public welfare. But consuming without producing is new territory for liberal democratic governments, and we have no developed guidelines that could prevent loss of core competencies and the creation of 'hollow state' structures. Contracting out central government policy advice roles (as recommended by Kemp, 1994) would give this potential for degeneration a strong extra spin (Boston, 1992). In Britain at least, Conservative ministers and the civil service elite have reached a meeting of minds on an absolutely clear-cut right-wing version of NPM. Essentially their current strategy aims to discover the core competencies of the state by a residualization process, outsourcing until and unless the shoe pinches, or a political backlash is triggered. Problems of protecting strategic non-core areas are estimated as minimal, but on *a priori* grounds only. Thus a 'mobilization of bias' highly favourable for the growth of large public services corporations already exists.

The Changing Context of State Policy Making

The implementation of NPM changes in the public sector is taking place in a wider international context which has already had some significant impacts on the capacity of nation states. A first, rather general influence has been the development of increased cross-national policy standardization as a result of a number of forces. Some critical public policy problems, especially those caused by cumulative environmental degeneration (such as species depletion, global warming, or oceans and fisheries destruction), have escalated past the levels where they can be effectively addressed by any nation state, however large. Increasingly the development of advanced technologies and the multinational corporate economy have also caused a scale escalation of issues as mundane as the design of cars or as complex as genetic manipulation.

These pressures have created powerful displacement effects, pushing issues up to a huge variety of supranational bodies, some multipurpose and others focused on single issues, some global and others regional blocs (see below). The much-reduced timescales for international policy learning also imply a progressively stronger pooling of ideas amongst liberal democracies, breaking down national insulation and distinctiveness on a wide range of policies, even on traditionally national-specific policy areas such as welfare state management and microeconomic support (Rose, 1993).

The second much more specific impact on nation states has followed from the growth of regional or sub-global blocs, such as the European Union (EU), the North American Free Trade Area (NAFTA) and possibly the Asia-Pacific Economic Council (APEC). These organizations have developed both in terms of the numbers and range of countries involved, and in terms of the scope of pooled decisions made or at least influenced at bloc level. The trend towards regionalization reflects in an institutionally systematized form the general pressures for upward policy displacement noted above, together with the concentration of trade and economic development into more spatially linked sets of countries than (say) two decades ago.

These pressures interact with particular force in the case of national governments in small- or medium-sized advanced industrial states, particularly in Europe where effective control of many economic decisions has formally shifted away from the national level to the EU (with global fora important in additional policy areas). National governments' roles in formulating independent economic and industrial policies have progressively been reduced, either by successive crises of macroeconomic management (as in the UK) or by a slower seepage away of industrial policy competencies despite public ownership efforts (as in France). Across north Europe some central governments have responded to their loss of functionality by moving out of fraught or failing efforts to retain nation state capabilities in international affairs or economic direction. Instead political controversy and attention has been concentrated on areas where the prospects of policy success offered by new public management agendas seem greater, especially micro-managing welfare state policies previously left to sub-national governments.

The EU has already called in question previously accepted features of 'statehood'. The EU treaties clearly limit member states' ability to control entry and exit from their territories. Member states no longer act as independent actors in some key international negotiations (such as the GATT talks), so that the EU seems to be accepted as a 'state' in this context by other states. A range of more subtle effects has also become evident. For example, EU institutions (such as the European Court of Justice and the European Commission) have reduced the unitary character of member state institutions, qualified member states' monopoly of authoritative decision making, and tended to erode member states' legitimacy in distinct policy areas. The links between populations and territories have also been blurred by labour mobility and European proto-citizenship provisions.

For the rest of the 1990s the rule making activities of the EU are likely to have substantial effects in opening up public procurement systems to 'single-market' disciplines and forces (Cox, 1992). Existing provisions have already produced a substantial shift in patterns of European business organization in relevant service industries, which successive privatizations of public enterprises promise to push ahead. The effects of these changes will work through diverse pathways, some in the corporate economy in terms of company mergers, acquisitions and internationalization, and some inside the conventional public service apparatuses themselves, in terms of the erosion of cultural and linguistic barriers defending 'national' domains. The ability for EU citizens to gain public service jobs in any EU country has important complementary effects here, together with the progressive Europeanization of university education systems.

CONCLUSIONS: THE WITHERING AWAY OF THE STATE?

If governments indeed pursue a strategy of searching for their core competencies by a residualizing process of radical outsourcing, what end results can we expect? Different answers are possible. The Quinn thesis insists that the 'best in world' criterion does not create 'hollow organizations', but instead a lean corporation tightly focused on its core competencies. Yet the grounds for expecting governments to pass this criterion (rather than a 'best in region' or 'best in locality' test) are weak, raising a real prospect of creating 'hollow government' systems. British privatizers argue that government's role will become one of simply being 'an intelligent consumer', a kind of purchaser-in-chief, with the private sector monopolizing all provider roles. Government would continue in a stunted form not as a proactive, strategic planner and service innovator, but as a mediating agency condensing the influence of citizen-consumers in areas where collective action might otherwise not be effective. Government's role is simply to react to and scrutinize innovations made by private corporations and decentralized nets of implementing agencies, rather in the way that in the past it organized defence procurement or drugs policies for public health care systems. The potent role of corporations and professionalized policy communities in distorting public policies in such areas in the past is apparently not seen as a source of problems in future public service production.

There is no technological determinist push in my account. It is worth stressing that the changes which have occurred so far and will occur in future are the product of a conjunction of forces – social, economic and political, as well as technological. And possible countervailing trends towards the creation of corporate domination of future public services markets can be identified. The advent of more humanized, in-house versions of NPM strategies is possible, dethroning financial cost efficiency as an overarching virtue and reinstating more developed notions of governmental effectiveness and social welfare maximization in its place. Governments may develop improved modes of running dual structures incorporating conventional public administration operating on legal/juridified lines and a 'shadow state' run on principal/agent lines (Garvey, 1992). And opportunities may develop for socializing and democratizing both the complex structures created by NPM strategies, and regional bloc structures such as those of the European Union. A restatement and restabilization of nation states' roles and the evolution of authentic, democratic conceptions for the guidance of supranational institutions is always possible.

But unless these countervailing forces become much stronger than they are at present, there is a clear danger of the radical outsourcing evangelism coinciding with bureaucratic incentives for organizational reshaping and political loss of confidence in the nation state as an expression of the collective life of complex societies. Taken together they may yet help to set in train significant steps towards the withering away of the state, or something like it.

The job of futurists has always been to connect two and two to make five. A wide range of intelligent speculation already exists in which by extrapolating current trends the role of the state is projected to reduce radically, or to disappear altogether in favour of new forms of corporate feudalism. To take a particularly graphic and dramatic example, in her science fiction novel *Body of Glass* the feminist author Marge Piercy envisions a future world where government functions have atrophied out of existence. Urban megalopolies have slumped into ungovernability. Multiple fiercely competing transnational corporations dominate the economy, and maintain their own company enclaves (edge cities and regional zones) for professional elites. The collective life has shrunk to a worldwide computer network essential for economic exchange and information sharing. Only a few small towns living on their entrepreneurial wits survive in the interstices between a corporately controlled culture, the major economic actors and an urban lumpenproletariat organized by large gangs. All this takes place against a background of extreme environmental decay, maintained in a perilous equilibrium only by a draconian 'environmental police'. It is easy to dismiss such fictional accounts. But as I noted above, forty years ago it might have seemed almost as incredible that there could exist worldwide restaurant chains. Some unlikely extrapolations are worth taking seriously.

3 The National Performance Review: A New Humanist Public Management?

Helen Margetts

The National Performance Review was the Clinton administration's version of New Public Management reform. Based on an intensive six-month study of the federal bureaucracy during 1993, it was predicted to save $108 billion and reduce the federal workforce by 152 000 between 1993 and 1998. The Review envisaged the reorganisation of agencies, reform of the budgeting and procurement processes and extensive reduction of internal regulations. The first section of this chapter outlines the reform efforts of Clinton's most recent predecessors, the second section looks at the recommendations of the National Performance Review, and the third evaluates their progress. Two years since the Review took place, many of the recommendations have been passed and the planned staff cuts have been increased. Will the NPR have any lasting effect on the federal bureaucracy or was it just a public relations gimmick that failed? The fourth section covers the second phase of the National Performance Review, announced in 1995, stressing privatization and government by other means in contrast to the first phase. NPR II has complicated the academic dialogue provoked by the National Performance Review; the accusation that the reform lacks a coherent or sustainable theme, versus the more optimistic view that the Gore initiative may be 'one of the most important things that Clinton does' (*Washington Post*, 13 September 1994). While the conventional view emphasises Congressional influences on bureaucratic reform, it is argued here that bureaucratic enthusiasm has institutionalized the first phase of the reform effort, rendering it successful in comparison with previous presidential attempts to produce lasting change. It is too early to establish whether 'NPR II' has any philosophical coherence, or whether it is a hurried response to the Republican Right. Certainly, NPR II illustrates the cross-national pressures for competition from which the United States is not exempt. But it is important to distinguish between the two stages of reform. In contrast to UK reforms, the first phase of the NPR has provided a vision of what a more humanist version of the New Public Management might look like.

RECENT HISTORY OF FEDERAL ADMINISTRATIVE REFORM

In Washington the announcement of intended civil service reforms is almost as frequent as the arrival of new presidents. These reform plans have a

47

common feature; they have been largely unsuccessful. Fewer of their recommendations have been implemented than have lain on the table to be incorporated in the reform plans of later presidents. Plans for administrative reform have had many other features in common. All previous reform plans were economy and efficiency based. There has been no equivalent of reform on the depth or scale of the UK Next Steps, but many presidents have used managerial strategies. Contracting out has been a feature of federal government throughout the twentieth century:

> Within a societal context overtly hostile to big government, contracting out government consumption and capital investment on a huge scale became a key element in securing political acceptance of a 'Leviathan' state. (Dunleavy and Margetts, 1994, p. 18)

Eisenhower, Kennedy, Johnson, Nixon, Carter and Reagan all brought investigative teams into the government seeking to transplant private sector techniques. Their efforts were usually founded in a distrust of bureaucracy in general and of the Washington establishment in particular.

Carter especially hated the Washington establishment, describing it as a 'horrible bureaucratic mess' (Massey, 1993, p. 88). On coming to power he immediately set up a Reorganization Committee. The committee consisted initially of a small permanent staff within the Office of Management and Budget (OMB), but quickly grew to around three hundred voluntary outsiders and agency representatives. They concluded that the federal service was 'unnecessarily complex, unrepresentative of society, inefficient and unaccountable, unable to reward merit and excellent performance' (Massey, 1993, p. 89). In response to their findings Carter proposed the Civil Service Reform Act which contained a clear commitment – albeit never fully funded – to performance pay and merit bonuses, and created the Office of Personnel Management (later used by Reagan for implementation of his own reforms) to oversee personnel policy. He also reorganized audit and investigation units within agencies and departments into single-headed 'Offices of Inspector General' under the Inspector General Act of 1978. The Inspector Generals were given broad and considerable powers to review legislation and regulation and to promote the economy and efficiency and effectiveness of their departments (Light, 1993, p. 23).

Carter also made an attempt at zero-based budgeting (ZBB) which in its purest form would mean agencies redesigning their budgets from zero every year rather than working from last year's expenditure levels. Carter's modified form of ZBB, which he had used while governor of Georgia, meant that agencies were required to prepare alternative budgets for each program based on different levels of effort in comparison with the previous year. But, as in Georgia, the idea was never really implemented. Agencies continued to work backwards or forwards from their current budgets. ZBB did influence the bureaucracy to some extent with more sophisticated justifying of increases but there was no evidence of substantial spending reductions or significant funding reallocations across departments. Moe (1992, p. 43) summarized:

> Reorganisation, first viewed by Carter and his associates as the route towards both efficiency and governmental virtue, by the second year had degenerated to the status of a tool for gaining interest group support for the Administration generally.

While Carter 'delighted in the minutiae of policy management' (Massey, 1993, p. 90), Reagan had little interest in the intricacies of bureaucracy. His reforming zeal was based around the view that the less government the better and his first act was a federal hiring freeze. He created a commission of corporate executives, chaired by an industrialist, J. Peter Grace, to increase government efficiency. The Commission consisted of thirty-six task forces composed of entirely private sector personnel, staffed by two thousand people generally on loan from their corporations. It cost the equivalent of £70 million. Its legal status was questionable (Moe, 1992, p. 45). The Grace Commission's reports contained 2478 recommendations with a potential saving of more than $424 billion, designed 'to get government off the backs of the American people' (Grace, quoted in *Dow Jones*, 8 September 1993).

Like the Carter Reorganization Committee, the Grace Commission rejected the idea that any principles of organizational management were unique to the public sector. Government should be organized like a large corporation with a structure permitting top-down control. Decisions were to be brought to the top into a large new office of Federal Management. Privatization through contracting out was seen as the most effective way of saving money. Blanket targets were introduced, whereby agencies were commanded to privatize 3 per cent of their operations. Some ($195 billion) of the savings were to come from a 'full-scale war on waste, fraud and abuse' (Light, 1993, p. 102). Reagan fired all the Inspector Generals created under Carter and recruited largely new personnel to fill their posts. These new Inspector Generals reached a pinnacle of power during his presidency but their focus on short-term statistical results resulted in enhanced reporting on waste rather than recommendations for management improvement.

The Grace Commission report was criticized by both the General Accounting Office (GAO) and the Office of Management and Budget (OMB). A large proportion of the Commission's detailed recommendations had already been made by career civil servants or in GAO reports. Seventy per cent of the recommendations required legislative approval and Grace drastically overestimated their chance of success. In fact very few of those recommendations requiring Congressional support were implemented, an unsurprising result considering the virulent criticisms of Congress contained in the report. Staff cuts were implemented with a 'meat-axe' approach and eleven thousand employees were laid off during the first year. Reagan's political head of the Office of Personnel Management declared 'war on the bureaucracy' and politicization of this organization contributed to 'fear, paralysis and sagging morale' (Gormley, 1989, p. 32). There was no attempt at deep-seated structural reform.

Reagan considered the budget the key to his overall objective. His plan, initially implemented by his budget director David Stockman, was to bring budgeting decisions to the top and reduce the part played by agencies, especially at the lower level, in the budget making process. In fact however, the executive budget process remained largely intact. As one official interviewed put it:

> In the first years of the Reagan administration the emphasis began to shift much more to central budgeting and with less emphasis on agency requests – although that process has never stopped. To this point they have continued the traditional bottom up process, it has never gone away.

The only notable change was a far greater amount of 'Congress watching' by agencies as they tried to avoid the worst effects of the cuts. Budget offices and departmental secretaries became reliant on methods such as 'dead-on-arrival' budgets, whereby they were content to include zero appropriations for White House targeted programmes, confident that Congress would restore them and thereby help push their department's budgets back over target. Budgeting strategies based on the belief that no one (especially government officials) could be trusted, resulted in a ratcheting upwards of caveats and control apparatus reminiscent of Downs' 'law of counter-control' (Downs, 1967). It has now become evident that none of Reagan's strategies were successful at reducing public expenditure. Cogan and Muris (1990) characterize the period as one year of deep budget cuts in 1982, followed by seven years of rapid budget growth which restored the aggregate domestic discretionary spending to its 1981 constant dollar level.

The administration changed little during the Bush period. Bush provides one exception to the reforming zeal that characterizes the first eighteen months of most presidencies. Administrative policy was a small and unimportant part of the neglected domestic policy arena. The most notable change that took place was due more to his Budget Director, Richard Darman, head of the Office of Management and Budget. Under his control the top-down budgeting that characterized the Reagan years reached its pinnacle.

In the agencies and departments resentment and frustration built up over how their budgets were developed, while in the White House itself, OMB became the only policy making organization that could influence the budget process, causing discontent amongst other White House staff. In 1986 Charles Levine warned of a 'quiet crisis steadily but surely eroding the capacity of the federal government' which 'if left unattended could produce major breakdowns in government performance in the future' (Kettl, 1995, p. 23). In short, Clinton's inheritance included a burgeoning deficit, increased internal regulation and controls and a largely frustrated federal civil service.

THE NATIONAL PERFORMANCE REVIEW

Clinton put administrative reform on the agenda even before he was elected. He based his administrative proposals during the election campaign on the now internationally known book, *Reinventing Government* by David Osborne and Ted Gaebler (1992). The authors envisage a new form of 'entrepreneurial government' with increased competition in service delivery, devolved budgets allocated on the basis of outcomes and community oriented service provision. Their vision is based on the idea that in many cases policy decisions can be effectively separated from service delivery: 'separating steering from rowing', whereby government becomes a 'catalyst', empowering communities to solve their own problems. The book is based on experiences from US state and local government and provides useful, pragmatic solutions to the type of problems faced by the Governor of Arkansas. It is easy to see why Clinton was attracted by it and why it was useful to him in this role. However, it does not tackle the scale or scope of problems found in administrative control of the US federal government.

It was perhaps this realization that led Clinton to initiate the National Performance Review, an intensive six-month study of the federal bureaucracy carried out by 250 government employees. He placed Vice-President Al Gore in charge; Gore was both popular and in need of a distinctive role. He had a long-term interest in administration, especially relating to information technology. While Carter's micro-management of his reorganization project distracted him from the political realities of Washington, Clinton must have realized that the political problems of his first year, including introducing NAFTA and health care reform to a Democratic but still sceptical Congress, would prohibit him from day-to-day involvement with the review. Gore was widely praised by government employees for the time and tireless dedication he devoted to the review and the promotion of its findings. As one official who worked on the review put it:

> You have the vice president's personal involvement. Unfortunately vice presidents have been kind of invisible people in the past. And I think the president gave vice president Gore one job – go improve government. And I think he has a fire in his belly to do that.

The National Performance Review staff were divided into twenty-two teams, half of which looked at the major agencies while the other half focused on 'systems': organizational and management structures, budgeting, personnel, information technology, financial management, procurement, regulatory systems and program design. The Agency Reinvention Teams consisted of staff drawn from agencies other than the one their team was scrutinizing, to prevent problems when they returned to their normal jobs. Internal reinvention teams within all departments and agencies were also created, to scrutinize agency-specific processes in detail.

David Osborne, co-author of *Reinventing Government*, wrote the book-like report of the NPR's findings. His racy style and gung-ho approach is evident in the paperback version, which is decidedly easier to read than the output of the Grace Commission (whose output ran to forty-seven volumes spread over 1300 pages) or the Carter Reorganization project (the reports of which can only be found buried deep in the Library of Congress or agency archives). But as noted earlier *Reinventing Government* was of no practical use for dealing with the problems of federal reform.

Consequently, although the NPR 'main' report takes up and reiterates the Osborne and Gaebler themes, including much of their vocabulary, the status of the 'main' report text remained unclear. All the key recommendations presented at the end of the report were the direct result of the work of the reinvention teams and they did not relate directly to the snappily titled and evangelically written sections: 'Cutting Red Tape', 'Putting Customers First', 'Empowering Employees to get Results', 'Cutting Back to Basics'. This section focuses on these recommendations combined with interview evidence gathered directly after the NPR report was published and subsequent status reports to assess their future significance and chances of implementation.

Budgeting

Reagan's administration was characterized by his avowed intention to enforce top-down budgeting. But in reality the executive budget process changed little under Reagan, with the original bottom-up process remaining largely intact. At all levels of most departments, budget proposals continue to be prepared by agencies and bureaus and negotiated with the level above (for a fuller explanation of the executive budgeting process see Dunleavy et al., 1992).

One consequence of this, as the NPR team observed, was that agencies spent a huge amount of time throughout the year on the budgeting process.

One of the aims therefore was to encourage the agencies to spend less time on budgeting. The executive budget resolution formulated by the President specified agency-by-agency totals which would come from studying the functional totals with sub-function ceilings and targets for agencies in presidential priority areas. This resolution is now made known to the agencies earlier than before and the time when agencies start budgeting is later, so that agencies are not 'budgeting blindfold' as happened before. Agencies were encouraged to shed budget staff, but given the discretion to choose at what level this happens.

The NPR budgeting team observed the various processes for dealing with OMB and Congress and the avoidance strategies which developed within agencies under Reagan. An official described how the revised process would help remove some of these:

> There should be lessons out there for game playing. People can sit around the table saying: 'This is honestly what we have, how are we going to divide that up? And we have discretion within the department to divide that up so OMB is not going to be second guessing.' So there is going to be less incentive for games of saying 'OK: lets put more of this, lets put less of this area – we know they [the White House] care about that area and they will put it back in.'

Concurrently, there was to be a decentralization of the budget making process within agencies, in the sense that agencies would have more discretion to create their own budgets within the set limits. The aim was to encourage the agencies to 'own' the targets more than they did under Reagan or Bush. In effect, officials suggested that this objective heralds a move towards portfolio budgeting, where departmental heads are given discretion to budget among the 'portfolio' of agencies and bureaus under their control. The budgeting team held extensive talks with government officials from Australia, New Zealand and Canada where portfolio budgeting has already been implemented.

The changes outlined above meant a change of role for the Office of Management and Budget, used extensively by Reagan as an agent of top-down budgeting. OMB was criticized during the Bush years for their overt role in policy making, where budget examiners were perceived to be making policy decisions. In 1994 the agency anticipated the 'most fundamental change in the agency since its creation' (Kettl, 1995, p. 60) in a report based on the findings of the 'OMB 2000' Review team which conducted the 'most comprehensive self-examination undertaken by OMB in recent memory' during the summer of 1993 (OMB, 1994, p. 1). The principal premise of the report was that management was integral to the budget and vice versa, and hence the two functions should be integrated as far as possible. Former programme associate directors (PADs) now head Resource Management Offices (RMOs); 'new entities unlike anything known in OMB' (OMB, 1994, p. 4). Each RMO oversees a collection of agencies with related functions: National Security and International Affairs; Natural Resources, Energy and Science; Health and Personnel; Human Resources and General Government. This change will also facilitate the setting up of projects that deal with more cross-cutting agency concerns, another theme of the review. The old general management division will disappear. The A-11 form governing budget formats has been revised, requiring integrated management and budget processes and mandating agencies to incorporate performance measures into their budget recommendations. The role of the OMB budget examiners (for whom a new title is being sought), which has traditionally been to scrutinise agency budgets in intricate detail, has changed from an emphasis on line item budgets to a focus on performance measurement, through the already implemented Government Performance and Results Act.

The OMB 2000 report also focused on the relationship between OMB and the agencies, which had become increasingly antagonistic during the Bush and Reagan years. There is to be more collegiality between OMB and the agency heads and more involvement of the agencies at the highest levels. The OMB 2000 report claimed a 'new and improved relationship between OMB and the agencies', systematized through Management and Budget Reviews and aided by some agencies extending invitations to OMB divisions to sit in on their own internal budget processes. The report proposed an expansion of this improved working relationship; OMB is to be more proactive in working with the agencies to identify cross-cutting themes for the Budget. Agencies are to be involved earlier and more extensively in the budget process;

> the FY 1995 budget process was designed to engage the agencies *substantively* and *jointly* in finding creative ways to craft a Budget that reflects the President's priorities ... we have already heard selected agency reports that this new effort has improved relations significantly since it began last year. (OMB, 1994, p. 18)

The changes to OMB have horrified commentators who had been campaigning for an increased prioritization of management functions within OMB (for example, Moe, 1992 and 1994). Moe, observing that the NPR would 'decrease the authority, responsibility, and size of the central management agencies, particularly the "M" side of OMB' (Moe, 1994, p. 115), claims that the change 'represents the final act in subservience of management to budgetary priorities' (Moe, 1994, p. 117). But the 'M' side of OMB has always been weak (and open to much criticism from Moe over the years) and perhaps its demise is not to be regretted.

Procurement

The prominence given to procurement and contracting in the NPR report related to the considerable growth in time and money spent on buying goods and services. By 1993, the government employed 142 000 workers dedicated to procurement, recording about twenty million contract actions each year. They spent about $200 billion every year, $800 per American. Of all the 'system' reinvention teams, the procurement team made the greatest number of recommendations, twenty in all.

The attention that procurement received was also related to the realization that in many agencies the procurement process had become completely rule bound:

> So many and severe are federal procurement rules that they are often observed in the breach ... It should surprise no one that the rules sometimes get folded, bent or mutilated. Nevertheless, violations are not to be undertaken casually since every step of the contracting process must be documented. The documentation requirements generate elaborate paper trails. Although violation of procedures rarely leads to prosecution, the paper trails can be made to yield evidence of wrongdoing. (Garvey, 1992, p. 104)

In early 1993 a congressionally mandated review reported that more than six hundred laws controlled every aspect of defence procurement and added as much as 50 per cent to the cost of a product simply because it was being sold to the government. Perhaps the most notorious example occurred during the Gulf War, when the Air Force tried to place an emergency order with Motorola for six thousand commercial receivers, yet no procurement official nor company official could waive statutory requirements certifying that the Air Force was being offered the lowest available price. The problem was only overcome by the Japanese government buying the radios. The NPR uncovered hundreds of similar examples.

The burgeoning set of rules that must be rigorously applied meant that the procurement process was extremely lengthy. The average time taken to complete a major buy was four years. This problem was especially acute in buying information technology (IT) because IT-based products change rapidly with an average product life-cycle of around eighteen months. There were many examples in the report of idiosyncrasies produced by the procurement rules. For example, there were nine pages of specifications and drawings for the precise dimensions, colour and shape of any ashtrays bought by the government. The procedure for buying a personal computer included obtaining twenty-three signatures and took over a year. One official observed how procurement staff were judged purely on whether the process had been followed; evaluating the resultant product took a low priority. While contract divisions concentrating on procurement had proliferated in agencies, few staff were given the task of evaluation.

NPR recommendations were consolidated in the Federal Acquisition Streamlining Act of 1994, finally passed in October 1994. The Act covered 225 major provisions of the procurement law which were either repealed or modified. The threshold above which procurement have to follow the 1600-page Federal Acquisition Regulation (FAR) has been raised from $25000 to $100000. Such purchases account for 16 per cent of expenditure but 95 per cent of procurement actions. One of the NPR recommendations proposed that the FAR be converted from a set of rigid rules to a set of guiding principles. The FAR was compared with the Australian equivalent which is twelve easy-to-read handbooks. Penalties are to be introduced for frivolous protests by disappointed tenderers and contract negotiation is to be allowed to continue up to the point of a contract award, tackling two contributing factors to the strangulation of many large projects. There is a proposal to pilot an electronic marketplace, whereby vendors will be able to access the details of other vendors' prices and the details of all government purchases and adjust their prices accordingly. This system would replace the current process whereby the General Services Administration negotiates deals for, say, bulk purchase of personal computers which quickly become greater rather than lower than the market price, a phenomenon previously familiar to most federal employees as 'buying a 286 personal computer at a 386 price'. There was a commitment to recognize other factors besides price, to define 'best value' and provide regulatory guidance to buy on this basis rather than solely on price.

Deregulation

Many previous presidents have used an endless variety of strategies to reduce the paperwork burden on the public and on the private sector. Such efforts include the ironically named Paperwork Reduction Act of 1980 which committed a division of OMB (the Office of Information and Regulatory Affairs) to a continuous surveillance of all federal regulations. However, Carter, Reagan, their Offices of Management and Budget and Congress were all

exercise? Third, within months of the report's release doubts were expressed over implementation; did the 'follow-up match the fanfare?' (*The Economist*, 15 January 1994).

Reorganizing, Reinventing or Re-engineering?

Some of the recommendations simply represent reorganization of institutions that have become overgrown and unnecessarily complex over the years. One example was the Department of Agriculture, which operated 14 000 offices worldwide with more than 112 000 employees and 11 000 field offices. It was proposed that the headquarters operations should be reduced from forty-three agencies and staff offices to thirty, the headquarters staff of 11 900 reduced by 7 per cent. HUD officially closed its ten regional offices in April 1994, converting them to field offices or integrating them with existing field offices in the same location. In the Interior Department the Bureau of Reclamation has removed a thick layer of bureaucracy, two deputy commissioners and all five assistant commissioners. As well as removing agencies the reorganization created new ones, including a Farm Service Agency, Rural Community Development Service and a Food and Consumer Service, which amalgamates and simplifies the existing arrangements. Almost all members of the Senate Appropriations Committee who examined the proposals felt this reorganization was long overdue and the systems dating from the 1930s needed streamlining. Previous attempts had been unsuccessful: the office director of the Agricultural Stabilization and Conservation Service office in West Virginia was quoted as saying that his outpost had been told four times previously it would be closed but this time according to Mike Espy, the Agriculture Secretary, 'we really mean to do it' (*Washington Post*, 30 September 1993). Other reorganizations fared badly in Congress. Favoured departments were exempted from downsizing. Congress sabotaged the Department of Labor's plan to combine 154 federal job training programmes, housed in fourteen different federal agencies into a co-ordinated effort.

Although media attention linked NPR with the *Reinventing Government* book, the Review's detailed study of budget, personnel and procurement processes and internal regulation also reflected the re-engineering principal. This technique was popularized by Michael Hammer in a book called *Reengineering the Corporation* and widely used in the private sector. It is formally defined by Hammer as 'the fundamental rethinking and radical redesign of business processes to achieve dramatic improvements in critical contemporary measures of performance, such as cost, quality, service and speed'. Re-engineering concentrates on processes rather than structures. It recognizes that it is possible to change organizations via redesigning processes without destroying and recreating new institutions:

> Companies that earnestly set out to 'bust' bureaucracies are holding the wrong end of the stick. Bureaucracy is not the problem ... .The underlying problem, to which bureaucracy has been and remains a solution, is that of fragmented processes. The way to eliminate bureaucracy and flatten the organisation is by reengineering the processes so that they are no longer fragmented. (Hammer and Champy, 1993)

The NPR was criticized for 'missing the boat on re-engineering' (*Washington Post*, 14 September 1993), but the criticism turned out to come from a rival re-engineering consultancy. In fact, the organizational structures and leadership management systems team did look extensively at the concepts contained in the book and Michael Hammer was involved in the review, conducting seminars. The findings of the NPR report contained many examples of government processes that made sense originally but were by then causing increased transaction costs and employee frustration.

For example, the rule making process involved a long succession of hearings and reviews which can generate costly litigation. Because the Department of Health and Human Services, for example, was so slowed down by this process in the issuing of regulations, states had to introduce their own regulations without the benefit of federal guidance. Some of these state regulations were later overturned after federal regulations were eventually issued, leaving the states involved financially liable. The re-engineering section of the NPR report proposed that agencies made greater use of 'negotiated rule making', whereby representatives of the agencies and affected groups were brought together with a mediator before draft regulations were issued and before all sides had formally declared opposition. This procedure allowed informal give and take that could never happen in court or in a public hearing. When the parties did reach consensus, regulations were issued faster and costly litigation was avoided. The Environmental Protection Agency had already applied these techniques to the issue of emission standards for wood burning stoves; the NPR report claimed that standards were put into effect two years faster and with better factual input than would have been possible previously.

Savings

The original NPR report (NPR, 1993) stated that the enactment of recommendations would produce savings of $108 billion over the next five years. The savings from the overhaul of the procurement system were expected to save $22.5 billion over five years. An executive order entitled 'Streamlining the Bureaucracy' proposed the reduction of 100000 full-time equivalent personnel and the NPR called for an additional 152000, both over the next five years. As with budgeting reform there was no administration edict to cut personnel offices in every agency and 'every department is making the reduction in its own way' (spokesman for OMB, in *Washington Post*, 11 January 1994), in contrast to the blanket reviews of federal jobs introduced by Reagan. By October 1995 $63 billion of NPR's $108 billion savings were enacted and federal employment had dropped by nearly 100000. Agency reinvention actions undertaken beyond the recommendations made in the original report would bring an additional $10 billion, according to the 1995 status report. The termination of federal subsidies for wool and mohair had saved $695 million. Congress has written into law that federal employment, now at 2.1 million, can be no more than 1.88 million by the end of fiscal 1999. The job cuts specified under NPR were raised by Congress to 272900 between 1993 and 1999.

Criticism of the proposed savings and personnel cuts came from all sides and ranged from 'too little' to 'too great'. Government employees expressed concern that they were too high. One official who worked in the NPR suggested that confusion had been caused by lack of information and fears of redundancy and that the cuts could be made largely through normal staff turnover and early retirements:

> People are focusing on the downsizing of federal personnel. Everyone thinks 'That's me!' ... When I went back to my agency they all thought it was them. And I said 'None of you are managers; this is directed at managers.' The downsizing is not really that great, it includes the 100,000 that was already published last year in executive order ... It is a seven year period through from '93, which is less than two per cent per year. We nearly get there by attrition.

Most of the employee reductions were made through buyouts. In March 1994 Congress authorized domestic agencies to offer cash bonuses of up to $25000. Nearly 15000 civilian federal employees had left the government through the buyout programme by November 1994, with 62000 in defence. And OMB approved 6500 buyouts in civilian agencies for 1995. Buyouts were popular and, according to the director of OPM, built on successful private sector experience.

The calculation of savings have provoked continual disagreement between the Office of Management and Budget and the Congressional Budget Office (CBO). In October 1993 when the Government Reform and Savings Act was passed, OMB claimed that there would be $6 billion in savings over five years; the CBO calculated the savings at $2.5 billion (Kettl, 1995, p. 19). Immediately after the announcement of the NPR, a CBO report recalculated the net savings at just $305 million from 1994 to 1998. OMB remained firm that their original estimates were valid. Eventually, by March 1994 OMB and CBO reached agreement (Kettl, 1995, p. 19). OMB have pointed out that the savings in most cases are not necessarily the primary reason for the proposed reforms: 'Perhaps the larger point is that these reforms ought to occur regardless of the scoring' (spokesman for OMB). Gore put it this way (*Business Week*, 13 September 1993):

> We will have significant savings. If you reinvent in the right way, you're going to save significant sums. If cutting spending is all you're interested in, you are going to make mistakes, and you won't get a transformed system of government. If you take a meat axe, all you will do is create tremendous anguish.

Before the NPR report was released, debate had focused on whether the report should be judged on its savings potential at all:

> There was a big fight in the White House over whether to address reinventing government in deficit-reduction garb or suit it up in good-government clothing. The decision was made that politically it would not fly unless it were wearing deficit-reduction finery. (Congressman in *Washington Post*, 13 November 93)

The NPR document had pointed out that private sector companies usually need six to eight years to transform their operations and the report should be viewed as a 'downpayment' on reinventing the bureaucracy.

By 1995, however, the debate focused around the ever-increasing emphasis given to the savings aspect of the reform. As David Osborne said in December 1993 'the trap [the administration] has to worry about is downsizing and making the government work worse' (*Washington Post*, 13 September 1994) which is conceivably what has happened at the Postal Service where service quality has plummeted. There seems evidence that cuts are coming before streamlining rather than the other way round. There were accusations that 'savings became the driving theme' (Kettl, 1995, p. 20), perhaps understandable given the importance of convincing the bureaucracy-hating American public that something significant really would happen: 'the figure captured the imagination of many people in the public as well as in the media' (Peters, 1994, p. 14).

Implementation

It was evident to anyone in Washington at the time of the NPR's release that implementation would be a problem. One official explained this as follows:

> The review process was a roller coaster ride of direction and mis-direction and 'go that way' and 'wait a minute go back that way'. And every day it was a new direction. We were more focused on getting the recommendations down and then letting other people later on think about implementation.

The NPR office was reduced from two hundred and fifty, to twenty-five personnel within a week of the summary report being launched and before the detailed reports came out. One official was back in her agency for just three hours before being asked to return to the NPR office for a further six months. Given the staff reductions proposed in the report and the heavily scrutinized, press-sensitive world of Washington politics it was hard to deploy personnel to implement the report when any increase in personnel in regulatory units in central agencies would be politically embarrassing. The chief institutional lever was to be a new President's Management Council, chaired by the Deputy Director for Management of OMB, which included officials from eighteen major agencies and the heads of GSA and OPM. It launched quality management 'basic training' for all employees, starting with top officials and cascading through the entire executive branch. But the President's Management Council was not permitted a significant increase in staff. The implementation plans were based on principles of cultural osmosis rather than on any institutionalized driving force.

However, the evident support of the White House cannot be accused of 'beginning and ending with a press release announcing the creation of a commission or task group to conduct a comprehensive and ambitious effort to improve management or reduce costs', as Harold Seidman (1993, p. 2) suggested it might. Gore's enthusiasm for what the *Washington Post* called 'one of the most unglamorous jobs in town' (14 September 1994) seems undimmed. He continued his rounds of federal agencies to observe and encourage their reinvention efforts: 'I've just about completed my second one. I'll be starting then on the third as soon as I complete the second' (*Washington Post*, 14 September 1994). While Clinton's popularity plummeted during 1994 and the first half of 1995, Gore's seemed more resilient. As Paul Light observed 'Vice-Presidents generally do worse than their Presidents, but Gore appears to be the Teflon Vice-President' (*Washington Post*, 2 October 1994). Perhaps part of his popularity is based on whatever success the NPR has had and his evident and continuing commitment.

Many of the recommendations could be implemented by executive order alone. In some cases the internal regulations identified in the report had been imposed on the agencies by themselves. One NPR official observed that:

> What we have found many times is that, even though there's legislation that's kind-of the original culprit, then you see that all the way down the line the agencies have added layer and layer of bureaucracy. The 23 signatures to buy a PC had nothing to do with Congress.

Thus many of the recommendations relating to procurement were implemented relatively easily, provided that the process of disseminating information about the recommendations penetrated deeply and widely enough into the bureaucracy.

The proposals which required approval from Congress have suffered a more turbulent ride. Both Carter, who was more interested in administration than politics and Reagan, whose Grace Commission report was littered with criticisms of Congress, misjudged the extent to which Congress would block their proposals. Early optimistic observations that the relationship between the Clinton administration and the appropriations committees was improving (Margetts, 1994) were not long lasting. In October 1993 the proposal to eliminate mandated minimum personnel levels in many departments or agencies was passed by both the House and the Senate: previously these lower limits had ensured that Congress could block personnel reductions. But relations were strained during the passing of the 1994 budget, when the full House approved only $8.8 billion (53 per cent) of Clinton's investment spending programme for infrastructure, expanded education and job creation programmes. The NPR teams had tried to establish levels of Congressional support for recommendations; for example, the recommendation for biennial budgeting was based on research done by the Joint Committee on the Organization of Congress which found that 70 per cent of Congress members favoured biennial budgeting. But legislation relating to the budget had an especially difficult time in Congress. Biennial budgeting met the same fate as an earlier Department of Defense attempt, consistently rejected by Congress, anxious that two-year budgeting would reduce their opportunities between elections to appease constituents with appropriations that benefit their own constituencies. Another recommendation requiring legislation was that agencies would be permitted to roll-over 50 per cent of their unobligated year-end balances in annual operating costs to the next year. If passed this change might have stopped the current 'year-end spending sprees' by agencies, anxious to avoid having to return the excess from unspent line items in their budgets. The NPR team received more examples of this source of waste – in letters, in calls and at town meetings – than any other. But this recommendation also languished in Congress.

However, by October 1995, 22 per cent of the NPR's recommendations requiring Congressional action had been signed into law. In some cases agencies did not wait for legislative approval. Legislation to end GPO's control over government printing, after sharp criticisms of its monopoly in the NPR report, was not passed, but many agencies started printing documents themselves, causing GPO to close offices and implement an emergency layoff plan.

The NPR created 135 Reinvention Teams and Laboratories in departments and agencies, allowing one element of reinvention to be completely decentralized, free from reliance on Congressional or executive actions. Initiatives within agencies have varied widely, depending on the momentum gathered behind individual reinvention efforts. The Department of Agriculture actually increased staff reductions and office closures above the targets set in the NPR report (Ingraham, 1995, p. 8) and carried out restructuring beyond that passed by Congress. The Bureau of Reclamation has re-evaluated and changed its core mission and downsized by 20 per cent, eliminating SES and middle management positions and decentralizing decision making authority to field offices (Ingraham, 1995, p. 9). At HHS, change has focused on surveys of employees' ideas for improvement and employing consultants to proposed changes, without any formal action plans emerging. At HUD the reinvention team has been disbanded and monitoring of implementation is not occurring in any systematic way (Ingraham, 1995, p. 10). In some cases, reinvention has been added to major organizational changes already underway, for example at the Internal Revenue Service (IRS), which is involved in a major reorganization and computer development project. It is difficult to establish which actions by the IRS, if any, are due to the National Performance Review.

According to the GAO, 93 per cent of the NPR recommendations are underway. The pragmatic nature of the recommendations means that some can be implemented, while others remain on the table. As one NPR team member said, 'I would like to have all of it. But if we just got ten per cent I would be happy with what I had achieved.' Ten per cent would also be a higher success rate than the Grace Commission or the Carter Reorganization project.

NPR II AND PRIVATIZATION: RESPONDING TO THE REPUBLICAN RIGHT

The achievements of the first phase of the National Performance Review should not be underestimated. Some critics claimed that the legislative part of the programme would be blocked by a Democratic Congress and completely destroyed by the election of a Republican Congress in 1994. But the administrations have been successful in passing some legislative changes which many critics said at the time of the NPR would never be passed – for example, the cessation of mohair and honey subsidies and the reorganization of the Department of Agriculture. Other changes were achieved without the support of Congress. The lack of emphasis on privatization and the stress on trust and empowerment of federal employees distinguished the NPR from reform movements in other countries, demonstrating that some elements of the new public management may be implemented without those more damaging to public sector morale. The success of the first phase of NPR in achieving savings seems to corroborate existing evidence (for example, see Zifcak, 1995) that governments of the left may have more success in cutting public expenditure. Its humanist approach distinguished the NPR from the history of US central government reform and placed it in contrast with the changes undergone by the UK civil service over the last decade. Case related and pluralistic, it went with the grain of what was feasible.

The NPR had focused primarily on how government should work, not on what it should do. Privatization, a primary theme in most New Public Management reforms of the 1980s, was noticeably absent. Most of Clinton's predecessors had already used contracting out to a large extent. Under Reagan's administration, the Assistant Secretary of HUD (quoted in Massey, 1993, p. 109) outlined four distinct pressures for privatization:

1. Pragmatic – a more cost-effective civil service.
2. Ideological – liberal economics.
3. Commercial – more business for the private sector.
4. Populist – choice in public services.

In the first NPR report there is some evidence of the first and the last but not the second or third. Under Reagan and especially in the recommendations of the Grace Commission ideological and commercial pressures were paramount. Blanket reviews of in-house tasks and contracted out work took place, with agencies instructed to privatize at least 3 per cent of their operations every year. Although these efforts were largely unsuccessful in their intent to reduce operating costs, the effect was to impose controls which institutionally forced agencies to contract out work even where it was not cost effective. Ceilings were placed on full-time equivalent staff, while contracting costs fell under programme costs and were not restricted in the same way as employing government personnel. One recommendation made by the NPR budgeting team was to remove FTE ceilings on budget line items and to place limits on operating costs instead. The definition of operating costs was to be changed to include contracting expenses currently included in programme costs, removing previous pressures to contract out in order to keep FTE numbers below the ceilings. This new pragmatic approach to privatization was prevalent throughout the recommendations. As one interviewee put it:

> There is still some interest in privatization ... but I think it has lost its ideological thrust. There was a huge ideological thrust particularly during the Reagan administration, less so during the Bush administration and virtually none in the Clinton administration .... It would have to be on the basis of a pretty strong cost-benefit allocation. That is, its no longer the issue the government should *not* be doing this regardless of whether it is worth it or not. Now it is much more on the basis of cost-benefit. The change means that it does get less attention than it did during the Reagan administration.

By 1995, when the second phase of the National Performance Review (NPR II) was announced, this mild approach to privatization had been replaced by something more ideological and populist and more reminiscent of UK reforms. In December 1994 Clinton formally initiated Phase II of the work of the National Performance Review. Phase II contrasts sharply with the first phase, with privatization and contracting out brought to the fore. Concluding that the first phase had concentrated on the first three themes of the original NPR report: 'Putting Customers First', 'Cutting Red Tape' and 'Empowering Employees to Get Results', Phase II is to concentrate on 'Cutting Back to Basics', which has come to mean a refocusing and, particularly, a downsizing of federal activities. The introductory document emphasizes 'federalism concepts', that is the termination of activities at the federal level. The outline of Phase II specifies five ways to fulfil this aim (NPR, 1995a):

- *Service Termination*: reflecting a decision that a service need not be provided by the federal government; 'this option includes many federalism concepts'.
- *Privatization*: reflecting the sale of assets and related service requirements by the government. Examples include waste water treatment plants, airports, ports, bridges, parks and recreation facilities.
- *Quasi-Government Corporations*: instead of providing the service directly as a public good, the government opts to create a corporation

and a 'market where there is none today'. Amtrak is considered part of this category.

- *Creation of Public/Private Partnerships*: where the government may share in the ownership of assets and may share in operational responsibilities, for example, the Port Authority of New York.
- *Competition*: the outsourcing or contracting-out alternative.

It is unclear how far the marked contrast between NPR I and NPR II was due to the Democrats' disastrous electoral showing in November 1994, when Republicans won control of both House and Senate for the first time for forty years. One senior White House policy adviser claimed:

> These ideas were an important part of the President's thinking before November 8th, and we were already heading down this direction, but the election had the effect of throwing the ideas into higher relief, putting greater focus on them, putting us into higher gear. (*New Yorker*, 23 January 1995, p. 38)

The new Republican speaker of the House, Newt Gingrich, had been talking for some time of transferring the accrued power of the federal state to the states in the name of 'devolution', 'federalism', 'subsidiarity'. And by 1994, in the eyes of some commentators, Clinton was now 'urgently competing against him in what amounts to a governmental disarmament race' (*New Yorker*, November 1994, p. 33). In the words of Elaine Kamarck, now in charge of the NPR reform effort,

> This goes beyond devolution to the states. It devolves to the level of individual empowerment. It says to the people: Forget government. Forget those dumb programs no unemployed person likes anyway. Give people money. Tell them they can use the money to go to school …. It's about demassification. It's about individual empowerment' (*New Yorker*, 23 January 1995, p. 38).

While the first phase of the NPR had emphasized employee involvement, the second phase was more clearly 'top-down' and centrally directed. In January 1995 Gore sent a memorandum to all departments and agencies in the government asking them to justify every programme and function they performed, considering each of the 'government by other means' options in turn. By October, five agencies had analysed their activities along these lines. HUD was consolidating sixty grant programmes into three performance grants, shifting funding from 3400 public housing authorities to tenants, saving $800 million through attrition and buyouts and establishing the Federal Housing Administration as a government-owned corporation. The Department of Energy was to sell the Naval Petroleum Reserves at Elk Hills and Teapot Dome and sell uranium no longer needed for national defence purposes. OPM was to eliminate 1800 more positions over the next five years. The Department of Transportation will move air traffic control operations and its 40000 employees to a semi-public corporation as part of $6.7 billion package (NPR, 1995).

It is too early to say whether NPR II will be sustained, or will be abandoned if Clinton's current revival in popularity proves lasting. Academic debate over the NPR has focused on whether the original reform package contained any coherent theoretical theme (see Garvey, 1995; Ingraham, 1995; Kettl, 1995). NPR II, contrasting strongly with NPR I, evidently fuels the critics' claims that the reforms were incoherent. But perhaps the NPR can only really be understood in contrast to previous reforms. The ideological pressures towards private sector provision during the Reagan and Bush years led to a ratcheting upwards of caveats and control apparatus leading to regulatory strangulation; the bureaucracy that Clinton inherited was in need of a pragmatic, rather than an ideological, reform effort. Unfortunately, the very pragmatism of the NPR reforms created a theoretical vacuum, easily filled by the pressures perceived by the Clinton administration from the Republican right.

However, to relegate NPR to the status of the Grace Commission or the Carter Reorganization Project, demolished by Congress and quickly forgotten is to make the common mistake of forgetting the bureaucracy (Dunleavy et al., 1995). The NPR study uncovered the resilience of executive processes, for example the budgeting processes and strategies that survived the Reagan/Stockman and Bush/Darman years. If reinvention efforts have really been institutionalized into agency activities, as even critical reports suggest (for example, Ingraham, 1995), then the initiatives created are unlikely to die away. 'Many public managers, as eager as anyone to make government work better, quickly embraced the opportunities the NPR presented' (Kettl, 1995, p. 13). If NPR has managed to focus attention on processes rather than outcomes, then the reinvention laboratories will continue to play a useful role. The more frivolous emphasis on privatization is less likely to remain sustainable; it is fashionable now, but a failure of the Republican right in coming elections might herald its abandonment.

If a view of 'Congressional supremacy' is held, then the NPR will vanish into arguments over downsizing and the hollowing out of American government. But a view of the resilience of the bureaucracy suggests that the NPR will continue to initiate innovative reinvention efforts and a descaling of regulatory build up. Certainly, the second phase of the National Performance Review illustrates globalization pressures on governments to introduce the private sector into governmental activities. The current emphasis on privatization seems likely to sour the newly improved relationship between OMB and the agencies. However, either way, the first phase of the National Performance Review provides an example of what a humanist version of the New Public Management might look like.

4 European Union and Local Government
Michael Goldsmith

INTRODUCTION

This chapter focuses on some of the changes which the European Union has brought to British government and administration. Reflecting the current interests of the author, it centres essentially on the impact which the Union has had on local government, giving rise to what the author has called elsewhere 'the Europeanization of local government' (Goldsmith, 1993), though some reference is made to changes at central government level. Whilst the chapter provides an insight into the adaptive behaviour of both central and local government in the light of changes brought about by the creation of the European Union, it also raises other issues, amongst them the difficult question of accountability, both at national and local levels, for policies and programmes which are the result of cross-national deliberation and collaboration.

Clearly the development of the European Community and Union, together with the work of the European Commission, has had a major impact on the ways in which both British central government and the civil service conduct aspects of their business. Ministers and civil servants travel back and forth to Brussels for ministerial meetings on a variety of detailed topics, whether it be fishing quotas, some form of environmental regulation, the condition of beaches or a single European currency. Senior civil servants will expect to have had a spell in Brussels as part of their portfolios as they move up the promotion ladder, becoming familiar with the ins and outs of the COREPER process and of Brussels decision making generally on the way. As anyone who has listened over lunch to the conversations in a Commission restaurant will know, Brussels is a cosmopolitan city in terms of European Union politics, and civil servants working there will be expected to hold their own in more than their native language – and to understand the political nuances being expressed by each nationality.

Yet it is as well to remember that the daily business of government is still concerned largely with matters internal to the United Kingdom, even if it is wrong to assume that Brussels does not have some influence on our daily lives. That influence is likely to be felt at four levels of government. First there are what might be considered as the macro political decisions, which grab the headlines in the press, occupy Parliament, especially the Euro-sceptics, and involve the Prime Minister and Cabinet Ministers in extensive negotiations. Examples of such decisions would be those concerned with the future shape of Europe (the widening or deepening debate), the distribution of powers between levels of government (a federal Europe), and the speed of economic and social integration, including the single currency debate. All of these issues are of importance, but they are essentially of the major periodic type, coming mainly to the fore around such times as the agreement of the Maastricht Treaty in 1992 or the further treaty revisions scheduled in 1996. Meanwhile, relevant civil servants and ministers are likely to be involved in detailed discussion, drafting and negotiation with their counterparts across Europe and in Brussels over the form of what might become a finally agreed document.

The second level of impact concerns many policy decisions, most frequently taken on a sectoral basis, generally involving a Council of Ministers agreement. The most frequent of these are in areas like agriculture and fishing or on environmental matters, whilst topics such as transport and social policy, or competition policy also receive considerable attention. Press coverage of issues relating to these areas is generally not so good, but the policy decisions are more routine and their influence likely to be more pervasive. It is these policy areas which are likely to involve the relevant departmental civil servants in bilateral or European-wide discussion with their counterparts across Europe, and is probably the fastest growing area of involvement for such people.

The third level of impact is concerned with the implementation of policy. Much of this takes the form of directives and regulations issued by the Commission. They result from detailed negotiations between representatives of member states, who then have to see that they are implemented. The British have a reputation for tough bargaining over these details, but a good reputation for both their willingness and ability to see directives and regulations implemented – that is to abide by the rules once agreed. The same often appears less true of some of our European partners, who often appear more ready to agree to the principles involved but are less happy to pay attention to the details, and whose ability to oversee their implementation occasionally leaves something to be desired. Examples might include the willingness of the French government to prosecute French farmers who attack British lorries carrying imports of lamb, or of the Spanish government to tackle those of their fishermen who invade waters traditionally belonging to British fishing fleets. Little attention is paid to these matters until or unless a particular issue grabs the headlines – see for example the coverage given the future of the great British sausage; the condition of British beaches, or where some particular special interest is threatened by a change of practice. Given that British central government is largely non-executive, detailed implementation of such directives and regulations is most likely to occur at the local government or agency levels, as we shall see later.

The last level of impact from Europe, but by no means the least important, is the impact which follows from judicial decisions taken through the European Court. Such decisions can involve HM government in considerable cost and action, as is exemplified by changes resulting from Court decisions in such areas as the rights to pension and other benefits of part-time workers, as well as women's rights to equal pay and conditions. Court decisions such as these appear to suggest that the celebrated British 'opt out' from decisions on a social chapter may be less valid than originally believed.

In all these respects and at all these levels, events and decisions occurring in Europe involve both British central and local government, so that not only do Ministers, civil servants and MPs but also local authorities increasingly find that their daily lives involve dealing directly with problems raised in Brussels and Strasbourg. Because of this multilevel involvement, this essay focuses on the impact of the European Union on both local government and on British central–local government relations which can be seen as an interesting case study of the more general problems facing British government *vis-à-vis* the European Union. For some writers, especially those who talk of a Europe of the Regions or of a Europe of the Cities, the continued development of the Union is likely to see power shifting away from national governments towards the Commission or the Parliament, on the one hand, and to sub-national units – regions or cities – on the other hand. Such a view would fit well with the general objectives of European Union, with its concern for continuing political and social integration to follow the economic and legal integration already achieved in many areas of our daily lives. It is also a view likely to find support amongst the many advocates of decentralization and subsidiarity in Europe, or those who wish to see some form of Euro-federalism, or who want regional government for England and devolution for Wales, Scotland and Northern Ireland, even if it is currently not attractive to the present government.

But one has to be careful to keep normative beliefs and empirical observations separate in making an assessment on what will essentially be one of the key political developments within the EU over the coming years, and which will certainly shape much of the debate in the forthcoming 1996 treaty revisions. And herein lies the rub – namely that the EU is a treaty-based organization and not a sovereign nation state. In this treaty based Union it is still the nation state which is the driving force. The EU still largely has to move at the pace of the slowest and to accept what is essentially the lowest common denominator of agreement on policy amongst the major players – and in recent years such a position has usually meant Britain exercising an influence over the rate of change. Thus, for example, whilst within the Commission, DGXVI, the directorate responsible for regional affairs, has been pushing for greater sub-national involvement and for decision making to be decentralized down to sub-national levels (John, 1994b, p. 10; Martin and Pearce, 1994), by mid-1994, senior Commission representatives indicated that they were prepared to remain more firmly within the formally agreed terms of Maastricht, thus suggesting that the definition of subsidiarity is less clear-cut that some observers believe. In the British case the result has been to leave it for central government to determine what moves down to the sub-national level. There is some evidence to suggest that central government is seeking to tighten its control over local government in this respect. For example, Martin and Pearce (1994) report the way in which central government ignored the Welsh local authorities' efforts to agree a collective strategy in relation to ERDF funding. Furthermore, its efforts to shape the Merseyside Objective 1 bid resulted in the Commission returning the bid for revisions which seemed more in line with what the Merseyside authorities had originally wanted. The emergence of the single government offices has also seen efforts to tighten central government control over the bids going forward to Brussels, if the experience of both the North East and the North West is any guide. In this respect Anderson's assessment of the central government acting as a gatekeeper to the EU and as the guardian of the funds remains apposite (Anderson, 1991).

The continuing dominance of the central government is also suggested by the way it deals with the additionality question. Both the Commission and many local authorities believe that the latter lose out from potential EU funds, notwithstanding the claim made by central government that the funds (especially the so-called structural funds) are taken into account in the annual expenditure plans and grant settlements. But the dispute over the RECHAR programme in 1992–3, which resulted in considerable additional funds coming to the British coalfield areas to aid economic restructuring, was only resolved by the central government stepping down in the face of determined opposition from the local authorities concerned together with that of the Commissioner concerned, Bruce Millan. As a former Secretary of State for Scotland, Millan clearly knew how the central government sought to interpret the additionality rules and took the opportunity (given the new programme) to block the RECHAR funds coming to Britain until the government came into line. Even allowing for this minor victory – since RECHAR is really outside the main structural fund programme – it remains doubtful whether much has changed in practice. Two reasons can be advanced for suggesting why this is so. First, the Treasury wishes to continue its tight control over public expenditure and would under no circumstances contemplate a return to the more freewheeling days of the early seventies. Second, the government generally wishes to retain its control over the general lines of policy development over both local government and other local state agencies and can thus be expected to resist any moves which might either increase local autonomy or increase the influence of the EU on such policy development.

If we consider policy implementation issues, however, a different picture emerges, but one which itself is likely to be subject to change. The European Union achieves much of the implementation of policy through the production of Commission directives and regulations. Central government is heavily involved in negotiating the terms of such directives, and so on, which occupy much of the time of those civil servants who have to deal with Europe. Nevertheless, in pursuing such negotiations the government relies on advice from interest groups and professional bodies, including local government, as to the exact line it should follow. Because British central government is largely non-executant, it is in a strange position as far as the detailed implementation of European directives are concerned. It relies heavily on local government and on other sub-national agencies, even though formally it is central government which is responsible. Local government is heavily involved because four of the main areas most heavily affected – trading standards; consumer protection; public procurement and environmental protection (waste management and air pollution) are all mainline local government activities, even if they receive little public attention until something goes wrong.

This situation is likely to change in a variety of ways. First some of the areas affect bodies other than local government – all state agencies are affected by the public procurement rules, whilst bodies such as the water companies have to comply with the environmental protection regulations. The creation of agencies, together with the privatization of many areas formally under public control along with the development of many special purpose bodies operating at the local level, means that the process of implementing Commission directives and regulations is not straightforward. In reality it involves a complex network of different public and private bodies, with the result that it is more likely that many such directives are likely to be implemented in a negative way – prosecution for non-compliance for example – rather than in a more positive fashion in which the state agency or private body involved seeks to adopt strategies which would ensure Britain is at the forefront of developments in many policy areas. Two areas, both involving different bodies, would illustrate this point – the relatively poor quality of many of Britain's beaches (largely a local government concern) and the poor quality by EU standards of British water (a concern for the privatized water companies).

A second reason why the present situation is likely to change is that, given that it is central government which, as treaty signatory, is formally responsible for the implementation of EU directives, and so on, it will itself become more heavily involved. At the very least it will set up monitoring bodies to ensure compliance with such directives, and in the longer run, as John (1994b) suggests, it may well wish to take over some functions for itself, on the ground that it is easier for compliance to be ensured through one body rather than many.

Having said that, how successful it will be is as likely to depend on developments within the wider European scene than simply on whatever view the British government takes of matters. The creation of the consultative Committee of the Regions, the development of Brussels-based cross-national networks of local governments and the involvement of individual British local governments in *les affaires Européenes* mean that local government is much better informed about Europe and can draw on resources which may enable it to counteract governmental initiatives designed to limit its activities in that sphere.

So how does local government operate within the European context? Since the 1991 Audit Commission survey local governments have become more European conscious, with the majority of them now having specialist staff working on European matters. Indeed, by comparison with many other European countries, British local government is well prepared (Goldsmith and Klaussen, 1997). However, many of these authorities are essentially rather passive and at best reactive to European initiatives, despite the extensive publicity which the more proactive authorities receive. There is a tendency for most authorities to use their staff on a part-time basis with regard to Europe – something to which they give only a part of their time. Even where there are quite well established European offices, many of them are tasked with providing information to other departments, leaving the latter to develop any bids as they see fit or to interpret regulations and directives accordingly.

On this basis, the main departments likely to be involved are environmental health, which has major concerns with directives and regulations in the trading standards and environmental regulation areas; planning/economic development, with responsibilities largely relating to the structural funds, and those departments (legal, purchasing and financial) concerned with matters relating to public procurement. More recently, local governments are likely to have been monitoring European decisions in the equal opportunities and labour areas, both areas which can have an impact on the rights of local government workers.

But the more proactive authorities take a more positive and strategic view of Europe. Some, such as the former Strathclyde region, had a long history of activity within the European context, joining the Association of Traditional Industrial Regions of Europe (RETI) network at the time of its foundation back in 1984. South Wales is another area with long-standing connections with Europe, as are cities such as Birmingham, Sheffield and Glasgow. Despite the slowness of the British central government in responding to the reintroduction of Integrated Development Operations in 1986, Britain had several in place by 1990, including Corby, Birmingham, Manchester–Salford–Trafford (MST), Merseyside, South Humberside and South Yorkshire. Clearly the availability of the regional structural funds were and remain a major incentive for involvement – the 1992 British part of the Eurolog survey (Goldsmith, 1997) showed something like 60 per cent of respondents were competing for these funds.

What also characterizes these more proactive authorities is the fact that the staff they have working on European matters is both larger and more skilled, as well as probably being engaged full time on European matters. It will be this team which takes the lead on European matters, and its members will not only have some fluency in a second language, but also wide-ranging European contacts, both in other countries and in Brussels itself. The group will take the lead in putting together the bids going to Brussels, working with the other departments and other agencies who might also seek to be involved. Increasingly such bids involve not only partners across national boundaries, but also partners drawn across sectors, so it is not unusual to find local authorities bidding for funds together with private sector firms. Not only will such proactive authorities be bidding to the major structural funds, but they will also be aware of the opportunities which exist amongst a whole host of other funds, where with a little skill and the right partners, it is not too difficult to leverage out extra resources from the European pot. For example, Scottish local authorities have been successful in playing the European game, and the Welsh, with the assistance of the Welsh Development Agency have had past successes (Cooke and Morgan, 1990), though more recently central government has restricted the Welsh authorities' attempts to make co-operative joint bids. Against this, as both the Audit Commission and Eurolog surveys report, many local authorities do not appreciate what is on offer. Small, often rural municipalities in particular appear less likely to benefit from EU programmes generally (notwithstanding their possible Objective 5 standing), and as a result are less likely to evince an active interest in EU matters even at the elementary level of seeking funds to support a twinning arrangement. The 1992 Eurolog survey reported that whilst almost two-thirds of British local authorities had some form of twinning arrangement, only about 14 per cent had sought EU funding to promote such arrangements.

Notwithstanding this kind of outlook, an increasing number of local authorities are involved in the building up of networks and partnerships. First there are those who have joined with others in the UK for the purpose of forming some regional association, which can then be used as a basis for bidding to Brussels on a broader basis than can be achieved by a single authority. Some commentators; for example Roberts (1994), point to the absence of a regional tier, especially in England, as a major weakness for local government in its dealings with Brussels, but in parts of England, notably the North, West Yorkshire and Humberside, Merseyside and Greater Manchester, as well as in places like Devon and Cornwall, counties and districts have joined together to provide a broad base for dealing with Europe. By so doing, such groupings can then go on to the stage of joining trans-European networks, such as the RETI, which includes places like Greater Manchester, South Yorkshire and the former Strathclyde regions. Then there are the Atlantic Coast regions or ARC, which includes some of the south coast counties amongst its members.

The Eurolog survey reported that about 90 per cent of British local authorities co-operated with other authorities on EU matters, although it also suggested that only about a third at that time (1992) were involved in direct co-operation with municipalities in other countries. Much of this liaison work is undertaken by officials – again particularly by the European officers, but elected members are also often involved. Whilst some writers suggest that this is a form of creeping regionalism within England, for our purposes one of the consequences of this type of alliance is the increased ability it gives the partners to deal with a regionally oriented European Commission, whilst another is the blurring of accountability to which joint action by a number of local authorities is likely to lead.

There are also examples of city-based networks. They include Eurocities (a network of major European cities including Barcelona, Birmingham, Frankfurt, Rotterdam and Milan); the EIC middle-sized cities network, which includes places such as Brighton, Telford and Chartres amongst others; the Co-ordinated Action for Seaside Towns (COAST), which includes such places as Blackpool and Morecambe.

A third type of network is one based on a particular economic sector, such as the Coal Communities Campaign, which was led by Barnsley, Lothian and Derbyshire, and went on to link up with French, Belgian and German coal communities facing economic restructuring and successfully persuaded the EU to introduce the RECHAR programme specifically designed to help such areas. Other networks hoping to emulate something of the success of the CCC, but which to date have not met with the same degree of success, include AIRLINE, which brings together both industrial firms and areas in which the aerospace industry is strong; and MILAN, established in 1987, which links together motor industry areas and companies (Benington, 1994). Another example is the LEDA network which deals with local economic development in municipalities undertaking essentially small-scale initiatives, with the main British participants being places like Durham, Nottingham and Strathclyde.

The advantage to an individual authority of belonging to such networks is that it not only provides them with a wider basis on which to approach Brussels, but also gives them access to a wide range of possible partners when it comes to putting forward bids for EU support. A further advantage is derived from authorities being able to support what the Audit Commission referred to as the 'latest in Euro-chic', namely the establishment and subsequent maintenance of a lobbying and information office in Brussels.

John (1994a) reports the existence by the end of 1993 of some eighteen offices representing UK sub-national bodies in Brussels, and the number will have increased since then. As such British representation is on a par with many other European countries – John indicates that Germany also had eighteen such offices; France nineteen, and Spain eleven. The rapid growth in the number of such offices suggests something of the growing importance of Brussels to British municipalities, and clearly involves them in engaging in what Mitchell has usefully referred to as a form of micro-diplomacy (Mitchell, 1994). Examples of places with such offices are Kent, Birmingham, Nottinghamshire, North of England, Sussex, Devon and Cornwall, East Midlands, Grampian and Strathclyde. Many of them are effectively partnerships, linking together more than one authority, which has the benefit of cost sharing. The cost of maintaining a relatively small office (one officer plus clerical assistance) is about £120k per annum (John, 1994a, p. 3), and few places have an office the size of the one established by Lancashire Enterprises Limited, which at six is on a par with many of the well and longer-established offices from some other European regions and cities, such as the German *Lander* for example.

Lancashire Enterprises Limited (LEL) is a particularly good example of such a Brussels-based operation, reflecting the very proactive view LEL takes of Brussels. LEL was established in 1990 as the privatized economic development unit for Lancashire County Council. Its main focus remains economic development within Lancashire, but it undertakes work for a wide range of bodies, including many other local authorities. For example, it is involved with Manchester in training work, and has worked with the North East Lancashire authorities in securing economic aid from Brussels. But it also undertakes a considerable amount of consultancy work for the Commission itself, and it allows other organizations to use its Brussels office as a lobbying base. Whilst, as John (1994a) argues, such a range of activities might mean that LEL is less able to represent its main 'client' (namely Lancashire County Council), it can also be argued that this wide range strengthens LEL when it comes to understanding the Commission's policies, its decision making processes and its priorities. Few British local authorities, for example, have recognized the crucial importance of being able to shape Commission priorities – something LEL have understood for a considerable time. Being in such a position is likely to have its benefits: LEL's biggest success was the brokering of the management buyout of the former Leyland Daf works in 1993, the achievement of which not only depended on LEL's links to Brussels, but also its credibility with private sector institutions, particularly in the banking sector. Its record over the years in both sectors has generally been good.

Kent County Council is a good example of a single-authority-based office, (established in 1990), if only because, in partnership with Nord Pas du Calais, it successfully persuaded the Commission to alter interpretation of the eligibility criteria for the INTEREG programme. INTEREG promotes cross-border co-operation between regions/countries who share borders with other countries, and is a programme much favoured by the Belgians, Dutch, French and German regions. Originally such borders had to be land-based ones, but Kent was able to persuade the Commission to allow them to have an INTEREG programme with Nord Pas du Calais, largely on the basis that they at least shared the Channel Tunnel. Since that time Essex–Picardie have established a Brussels-based office seeking to achieve something similar, and the Yorkshire–Humberside has linked up with places like Rotterdam in attempting to promote its Green Links programme designed to development a West–East transport link across the Union and on into parts of Central and Eastern Europe. Another example is Birmingham, which has had an office in Brussels since 1984 (as has Strathclyde), and as a city is one of the most active in European networks.

As John (1994a) correctly notes, such offices undertake a number of functions. First, they provide a Brussels base for local authorities wishing to do business with the Commission. Even a shared office allows an authority to send individuals to meetings or to make phone calls, send and receive faxes, develop contacts, and so on, in Brussels in a way which is more difficult from the UK. Second, and importantly, the offices act as a listening post, providing information at an early stage to sponsoring authorities. The local representative is very much concerned with keeping abreast with new developments and current policy debates – and seeking above all else to gain early warning about any Commission initiative which might lead to some support or finance for the sponsor.

Third, as has been noted in the case of LEL, an important function of the Brussels office is to be able to lobby the Commission or Parliament in relation to either specific decisions or long-term policy – the pan-European networks and alliances to which local authorities belong can be given shape through Brussels, and action co-ordinated in a way not possible from a single authority. Meetings can easily be arranged, proposals and papers put together, bids developed at speed, Commission conferences and seminars attended, and evaluations made, both by the Brussels-based officer and through the Brussels network to which they all belong. In particular the Brussels-based office does help to build up the alliances and partnerships with other municipalities and regions essential to bidding and lobbying. It is this kind of coalition which gives authorities the opportunity to share and develop the Commission agenda and policy, often in co-operation with Commission officials, though the latter are always likely to remember the veto power of member state governments. Last but not least, such offices can be a source of information and assistance to other bodies – private sector firms, voluntary groups, and so on – and helping to make the European Union a reality for the sponsoring locality.

In part it is for this reason that the Commission has not been unhappy to see a plethora of offices and networks emerge rapidly over the last two or three years, in many cases providing some initial funding to help the networks get started. In other words there is something in the offices and networks which is mutually attractive to both the Commission and the worlds of regional and local government. Some directorates, such as DGXI with responsibility for environmental matters, both encouraged and found itself lobbied by networks concerned with urban environmental matters (Andersen and Eliassen, 1993; Mazey and Richardson, 1993). DGXII, with its interest in innovation and technology transfer through the STRIDE programme, encouraged similar developments. DGXVI, the directorate concerned with regional affairs, has been encouraging partnerships and networks in order to improve both the dialogue it has with sub-national bodies but also to develop policy implementation. Working with other DGs and their networks, DGXVI is often in the position of being a co-ordinating body, bringing together interests covering a wide range of topics and able to lobby accordingly.

One example of the way in which such a development has taken place on a wider scale is the creation of the Committee of the Regions following the Maastricht settlement in 1992. This is a formal EU consultative committee, which allows representatives from regions and local authorities to transmit their views and opinions on matters of EU interest. Since its creation, this body has been extremely active, establishing commissions on a variety of topics and submitting opinions on the future development of the EU itself.

The Committee is committed to trying to persuade the 1996 constitutional conference into granting sub-national government a more formal part in the policy making processes of the EU, and seeks to obtain greater clarification of the principle of subsidiarity in a way which will enshrine the role of sub-national government. It has been engaged in a dialogue with the former and current presidents of the Commission about future developments. It brings together almost two hundred elected representatives from all over the member states, with the twenty-four British representatives being nominated by the local authority associations. A predecessor body, the Council of European Municipalities and Regions, continues as a lobbying body for sub-national government, with considerable British participation. The Local Government Information Bureau acts as an information clearing house, listening post and early warning system on behalf of British local government as a whole, and maintains a small office in Brussels for these purposes.

All these bodies are essentially general bodies representing local and regional government as whole. What they are seeking to do is to influence the EU agenda, especially with a view to incorporating the world of sub-national government into the EU decision making processes. But, as the debate over subsidiarity and Maastricht demonstrates, such sub-national involvement means different things to different levels of government. Whilst for the British central government subsidiarity means keeping as much as possible at the national level, English local authorities would see greater recognition along Council of Europe lines as one way in which the yoke of central government might be loosened a little. By contrast the German *Lander*, amongst the strongest advocates of subsidiary at the time of Maastricht, were more concerned that without such a principle they would see their powers being taken up increasingly by Europe – and they certainly were not concerned with seeing German local governments being more heavily involved in European decision making processes (Wollman and Lund, 1997). Yet working with sub-national governments might be in the interest of the Commission and the Parliament, enabling them to by-pass those central governments who might interpret EU policies and programmes in ways not originally intended by the Commission.

The criss-crossing spiders' webs of intergovernmental networks which make up much of the real world of European Union politics also help the process of European integration, albeit if the various actors are bound together only loosely and perhaps rather fragilely at this point in time. But their very complexity mirrors that found in the rules which govern the implementation of European policy programmes, making the question of accountability still more difficult to resolve. Whilst local authorities seek European partners for reasons other than simply bidding for European funds, the rules of most funding opportunities require some form of cross-national and/or local partnership. Bids are put together by small groups of professionals, often in a flurry of faxes, with some of the work being undertaken from the Brussels-based offices of European networks – all a long way from the local accountability suggested by traditional models of local government. If local politicians know about these programmes, it is very much at second hand, and their support is based not so much on a sense that European co-operation is basically 'a good thing' than on a wish not to miss every funding opportunity the EU presents. The process of selection and support of bids, which also requires some national government input, is also complex and largely unseen by the public, whose first knowledge of an EU programme is likely to be sight of the notice board announcing a project at least partially funded with EU support. And when it comes to the implementation of European directives and regulations, life becomes even more complex and mysterious ...

Equally, accountability at national government level is difficult to enforce. On the one hand, for example, national government will take a stand on the main issues confronting the EU – monetary union, future membership, deepening the Union, and so on – and such debates receive national press coverage. Everybody is familiar with the British government's apparent isolation from many of its European partners on some of these issues: yet the reputation of the British politicians and civil servants who operate at the European level is generally high.

On the other hand, national governments will be concerned to see that they receive their fair share of European monies, encouraging sub-national governments and other bodies to make bids which lead to funds flowing to the country. Often it will be a case of the national government taking the lead, perhaps persuading reluctant or less skilful localities to bid for programmes for which they meet the eligibility criteria. Balme and LeGales (1997) suggest that such was the case with the French government on programmes such as RENAVAL and RESIDER. In these case central governments are pulling lower-level governments into Europe, rather than local governments themselves pushing at the European door. And again national governments may decide to take a stand against some European directives of judgements from the European Court. The Italians have a long record of decisions against their failing to implement EU directives and regulations, and even the British government, generally well-known for its acceptance of the rules once made, has expressed concern over some judgements by the European Court. And of course both local and national governments have come together to protect such consumer products as French cheese, German beer and the great British banger in the face of

European-wide regulations which would force changes in the mode of production or the complete loss of the product.

It is in the implementation of consumer or trading standards as well as in the field of environmental regulation that sub-national governments are most likely to become involved in the process of enforcing European-wide directives and regulations. The Commission in Brussels clearly lacks a sufficiently large force to oversee such implementation, and thus must operate on the basis of exception being brought to its attention rather than strict oversight of enforcement. Yet there is likely to be great variability in the way in which directives and regulations are interpreted at the local level, notwithstanding the provision of guidelines from the Commission, national government and/or relevant professional bodies. The introduction of particular directives or regulations is likely to give rise to extensive lobbying by various interests likely to be affected, both at the European and at national levels, perhaps leading to the capturing of the national level by specific interests, who persuade the government to exercise a veto on a particular initiative. Again accountability becomes difficult to enforce in this somewhat uncertain environment.

All this is of course part of the well known democratic deficit from which the European Union suffers. It is hardly surprising, given that the balance of power between Commission, Parliament, Council of Ministers, national governments, state and local governments and other agencies is constantly changing and where the link between elected representatives and voters is extremely weak. But accountability in this context is important for two important practical reasons: first, to avoid the inefficient and wasteful use of resources and, second, to ensure that corrupt practices do not exist. Unfortunately there have been sufficient reports to suggest that both the waste of resources and the presence of corruption as well as the illegal use of European funds are all part of European Union politics, in other countries if not within Britain. The introduction of EU guidelines for public procurement represents another area where accountability may be difficult to enforce and which may certainly lead to delays, notwithstanding the intention of making such procurement both more transparent and open to competition throughout the Union.

CONCLUSIONS

Institutional structural change of the scale involved with the development of the European Union necessarily produces changes in the behaviour and organization of national and local governments. Both the formal and informal rules of the game are constantly changing, and the three partners to the relationship are constantly seeking to maximize the relationship to their advantage. Brussels' gamesmanship, as seen from the regional and local government perspective, reveals that sub-national governments have not only developed the art of grantsmanship to a level not far removed from that of their North American counterparts, but that like them, they have also learnt the benefits of having good sources of information and a communications base at the political centre of Europe. Brussels is not that far removed from Washington in that respect, and the networks and offices which regional and local governments of all countries and political hues have established is evidence of that fact. Like good lobbyists in Washington, the better and more able regional and local government networks have also learnt the value of influencing and shaping the European political agenda.

Of course, in all this, and perhaps not quite like state governments in the United States, national governments in Europe continue to be major players on the European Union stage. Sub-national governments may be able to by-pass their national governments in some areas, but they know that their chances of success are much greater if they have the support of their national government when making bids to Brussels or seeking some policy change or innovation. And on the major issues, like a single currency, defence, as well as what might seem to be lesser issues such as fishing quotas, central government remains the major player involved in discussions. Member states are the main constraint under which the Brussels bureaucracy operates, notwithstanding its attempts to build coalitions both with the European Parliament and with sub-national governments and other interests, however dependent they may be on the latter when it comes to the implementation of policy.

What of the future? The 1996 treaty revisions increasingly seem likely to disturb institutional arrangements as little as possible, with a probable emphasis on broadening rather than deepening the European Union and with the single currency dominating discussions. Despite efforts by the Committee of the Regions to see sub-national government given a larger role in the formal procedures of the Union, it is likely that other matters will push this question off the agenda, though the subsidiarity principle may well be given another airing and some further clarification. The main policy instrument affecting sub-national government, namely regional policy, seems unlikely to be changed extensively until 1999, though there may be some different emphases within it. Issues like the environment, transport and the Information Society are all likely to continue to receive attention, and one might expect further initiatives, directives and regulations affecting these areas.

National government will continue to be largely concerned with the major issues concerning questions like European economic policy and enlargement of the Union. But the increasing amount of European regulation is undoubtedly going to bring some pressure on central governments to find ways and means of co-ordinating policy implementation, and one might well find the new regional government offices being asked to play an increasingly important role in this respect. The alternative would seem to be to increase the number of agencies expected to oversee this work.

Whilst a development of this latter kind might at least ensure some uniformity of action on relevant matters, there remain accountability dangers. Enlargement, as well as increasing European regulation, be it from the Commission or from the European Courts, are all likely to make accountability more difficult. Tackling this problem remains, and is likely to continue as one of the main problems of the burgeoning European Union.

5 The Automated State

Helen Margetts

INTRODUCTION

In the last forty years, information technologies (ITs) have come to play an increasingly major role in state organizations. Early computer systems replaced human labour in existing administrative systems, such as payroll and accounting. Modernization projects during the 1980s brought computers into the heart of administrative operations down to the local level. The spread of the personal computer and the development of network technologies made information systems available to even the smallest of departments and agencies. A variety of metaphors has been used to describe what this development means for the future of government; for example, the Virtual State (Frissen, 1995) and the 'Information Polity' (Taylor and Williams, 1992). These writers focus on the 'information' aspects of information technology, reflecting the observation that during the 1980s, 'automation, the computerization of existing practices, gradually is replaced by "informatization", a combination of information-management, organization and policies' (Snellen, 1994, p. 285).

The retention of the word 'automated' in the title of this chapter is intended to emphasize one particular aspect of the increasing role that computer systems play in state operations. Traditionally, the functions of the state have been exercised through the operation of large-scale bureaucracy. While bureaucracy was by no means unique to state organizations, it was generally regarded as something government was 'good at' and 'knew about'. As administrative functions are replaced by information systems, a significant part of government's organizational capacity involves a specialist task that policy makers know little about. Information technologies of the 1990s go beyond the mere replacement of existing functions, with technical developments such as virtual reality and increased access to the Internet offering new possibilities for policy innovations and an extension of citizen–state interactions. But the same characteristic is true of the additional policy possibilities available through such technologies; the method by which policies are implemented is increasingly opaque to non-specialist observers.

Within the growing body of research into the relationship between information technology and public administration now known as 'informatization',[1] Taylor (1992) argues that 'Rather than a focus upon automation, a concept which inevitably places technological considerations to the forefront, the focus should be on "information"' (Taylor, 1992, p. 376). The intention of this chapter is not to deny the use or importance of such an approach, but to return for a moment to consider some of these technological considerations of the history of government computing that the 'informatization' approach pushes to the background. It is argued here that the type of 'informatization' that state organizations adopt is crucially shaped by the technological decisions that they have made in the past. And control over these decisions, resting with those organizations that possess the technical expertise to understand both existing information systems in government and recent technological developments, will be a crucial function of the automated state in the future.

To illustrate how computer systems have spread throughout state organizations and how control over their development has changed over time, this chapter falls into five sections. First, the different ways in which information systems have come to play a key role in the 'tools' of government policy are examined. To an ever-increasing extent, these information systems are now designed, developed and operated by private sector companies. This development follows a similar trend in the private sector, examined in the second section, while the third section looks at the contracting out of information technology in the UK central government. The fourth section covers what will now be a key role for state organizations; the management of large-scale information technology contracts. The final section considers the impact of the decision to externalize government information technology for the automated state of the future.

INFORMATION SYSTEMS AND THE TOOLS OF GOVERNMENT

Government organizations were early innovators in building computer systems. From the 1950s computers spread across government and even by 1958 the former Ministry of Public Building and Works had adopted 'a very ambitious proposal for a computer-based system embracing all the routine work of the department, involving linking payroll, bill payment, stock control and vote and repayment accounting to facilitate the management of their resources' (Lamb, 1973, p. 125). By 1969 there were over 180 computers in the central civil service, over half in the Treasury and Ministry of Defence. In the early days, huge mainframe systems required resources that only the largest departments could command; such systems tended to be centralized in large computer centres. Some of the larger departments such as the Inland Revenue and the Department of Social Security undertook major modernization projects during the 1980s which brought computers into local offices and to the core of administrative operations. Also, during the 1980s the development of network technology and powerful personal computers with standalone computing powers and the network technology to link them together meant that information systems became available to smaller departments and agencies. In the 1990s, any investigation of the administrative operations of governmental organizations will reveal networks of information systems processing data about individuals, organizations, goods and services, carrying out financial transactions, registering authority and providing management information.

One way of viewing the centrality of information systems to governmental operations is to identify their relationship with the 'tools of government' in Christopher Hood's (1983) well known approach. Hood uses the division of 'detectors' and 'effectors' (derived from cybernetic theory) to describe the various ways in which government interacts with the outside world. Governments use detecting tools to find out about the world and effecting tools to make things happen; to make an impact. These tools draw on four basic resources that governments tend to possess by virtue of being government: treasure, authority, nodality and organization, and information systems now play a vital role in the utilization of these resources.

'Treasure' denotes the possession of a stock of moneys or that which can be freely exchanged. Detecting tools identify the financial resources of organizations and citizens, a crucial task of the Inland Revenue. Effecting tools use treasure to purchase goods or services or to give money away. Financial systems were the earliest systems to be introduced into government and every department or agency is now peppered with financial management, budgeting and accounting systems. Both the Inland Revenue and the Benefits and Contribution agencies have undergone large programmes of computerization and information systems are now crucial to their core functions of recording, processing and analysing financial transactions with individuals and organizations.

'Authority' denotes the possession of legal or official power; 'the ability to command and prohibit, commend and permit, through recognised procedures and identifying symbols' (Hood, 1983). The key organizations wielding authority in the two governments are the police forces and the immigration agencies, those agencies that have the authority to levy and collect taxes, and those that enforce licensing controls, such as the Driver and Vehicle Licensing Agency. Information does not alter authority itself, a distinctive resource which some governmental agencies possess. But there is great potential for information technology to fuel the exercising of authority by government agencies. The authority wielding agencies have been among the most innovative users of information technology. For example, computer systems in the Vehicle Licensing Office, the Home Office and police organizations play a vital role in storing information which is then used to assess what actions can be requested of individuals or organizations. Modern systems of regulation rely heavily on computerised information to assess whether, for example, the privatized utilities are carrying out their prescribed functions legitimately. The Home Office is now developing a national automated fingerprint recognition system, and in 1995 a system to check DNA became operational described by some commentators as the most dramatic development in criminal investigation since fingerprinting. The Customs and Excise department has developed a fully automated VAT collection system and drug control system and maintains the new systems needed for changing trade and travel rules in the Single European Market.

'Nodality' is the property of being in the middle of information or social networks. Government 'sees' many different cases and builds up a store of information; it is also in a unique position to distribute information to society. Information systems provide government with a greater capacity to use its nodal resources, by increasing the possibilities for storing and distributing information. The Home Office, the Benefits Agency, the Department of Transport and the Inland Revenue all contain databases of information about a large sub-set of the population, with ever-increasing capacities to process and analyse it. More recently, the Internet provides an ever greater variety of possibilities for government agencies to provide information to citizens and to businesses (on the Worldwide Web, for example).

'Organization' is 'a label for a stock of land, buildings and equipment, and a collection of individuals with whatever skills they may have, in government's direct possession' (Hood, 1983, p. 72). The impact of information systems on this tool of government differs in that information technology provides the potential to reshape organizational structures, creating flatter hierarchies, reducing the amount of staff required to carry out operations and facilitating the creation of infinitely replicable units. To some extent information technology takes over and reshapes the role that organization formerly played. Government agencies' lead role in information technology development up until the 1980s also introduced a new army of technically skilled personnel into governmental organizations. Hood (1983, p. 6) actually described the organizational resource as giving the government the physical ability to act directly, 'using its own forces rather than mercenaries'. But because, as discussed below, the development of computer systems is seen as a technically specialist task, unsuitable for government organizations, they are increasingly designed and developed by private sector companies. In this sense information technology has reduced the extent to which government uses its own forces and pulls new 'mercenaries' into the state.

The process of introducing computer systems into state organizations is by no means complete. In the 1990s, the technical possibilities for change in the operation of the tools of government and the reality of the automated state have diverged, evidenced by differences between possibilities realized in the commercial sector and in governmental organizations. With regard to treasure for example, it is conceivable that Social Security offices could disappear and the Benefits Agency could operate an entirely 'virtual' organization along the lines of VISA. Electronic filing of taxes, as introduced in the United States, is another option now technically feasible. In the Office of the Paymaster General a review in 1990 observed that the agency was unable to provide customers with an overall statement of all the transactions on their accounts due to incompatibilities between the Agency's two computer systems (NAO, 1995c, p. 9).

Future innovations rely heavily on interfaces with existing technological infrastructures, as the following example illustrates. When in April 1995 the Minister for the Office of Public Service and Science (OPSS) publicly announced his electronic mail address, a journalist sent perhaps the first electronic mail message to a UK Minister from a member of the public. At an ESRC/PICT conference on Information Technology and Social Change two months later, he asked the head of the CCTA, Roy Dibble, why he had not had a reply? Now that citizens were talking to government, when was government going to talk to citizens? Roy Dibble replied that the journalist's questions were currently sitting on his desk. When the Minister received the electronic message it had been printed off and sent to Roy Dibble by post. One of his staff had written to the relevant agency heads with a request for information; their staff would prepare this information and send it back to Roy Dibble's office where it would be collated and returned to the Minister's office. He would check the information and one of his staff would type it on to electronic mail and transmit to the journalist. This evidence of how new methods of communication can flounder when having to interface with existing administrative operations is not isolated; an employee of a Next Steps agency observed in 1995 that as a matter of procedure, all electronic messages sent to the agency were printed off and filed.

Thus the realization of the radical technical possibilities now available are constrained by existing technological infrastructures. Any of the innovations currently under consideration must be linked to existing systems; social security smart cards, for example, must update and be updated by the existing databases of the Benefits and Contributions agencies. Information systems are far more often modified or developed than replaced. Integration between existing systems is one of the key areas in which innovations can take place, meaning that past decisions create a rigid administrative inheritance. The nature of this inheritance is crucial as major possibilities for policy change will come from the matching of data and the integration of existing systems. The Benefits Agency is already involved in a long-term plan to rationalize the benefits system, involving the integration of currently distinct and non-compatible systems, the legacy of former systems development carried out in the 1980s. The possibility of merging the tax and social security systems, is a radical policy change that could only take place through mammoth systems development work on the computer systems of the Inland Revenue and the Department of Social Security; there are currently no links between the two systems, and any data transfer between the two departments is downloaded to magnetic tape and transferred manually.

Notwithstanding wide variations in the extent to which state organizations have made use of technical developments, if even a small proportion of the changes now possible are realized, it is evident that information systems will become an increasingly important part of any state organization. In the Netherlands, Snellen and Zouridis (1993) found thirty systems in ministerial departments which 'accounted for the whole or part of policy implementation in a certain field' (Snellen, 1994, p. 293). Furthermore, such developments are not neutral with respect to policy. Information systems have been found to reduce the separation between policy formulation and implementation, with implementation systems generating sophisticated policy relevant information (Frissen, 1994). Technical innovations that aid authority, for example the Police National Computer and the proposed national identity card, impact policing policies and have far-reaching implications for the control functions of the state. Computer systems can facilitate flexibility in policy making, for example through the more sophisticated means-testing of benefits or greater ease in the changing of tax bands. They can also reduce flexibility; the reason why the Chancellor sometimes announces tax changes so far in advance is due to the required timescale for the adaption of computer systems and the impossibility of keeping development work secret.

Those organizations that have an in-depth knowledge of the existing systems of government will therefore play a key role in the operation of the automated state. To an ever-increasing extent, the information systems that government uses are maintained, developed and run by private sector companies. Using a strategy now commonly known as 'outsourcing', government organizations have followed private sector companies in employing computer companies to operate their information technology. The following two sections provide a brief outline of this development.

THE OUTSOURCING OF INFORMATION TECHNOLOGY: PRIVATE SECTOR PRACTICE

In the early days of computing, both public and private organizations developed their own information technology systems. But as technology developed and the functions it could perform increased in variation and complexity, companies realized that they would have to become experts in IT development as well as their core business. Many turned to computer specialists and a burgeoning computer services market, increasingly populated by global players, has grown rapidly to meet demand, with the leading vendors as shown in Table 5.1.

Table 5.1: Leading Vendors in the UK Computer Services Market
(Public and Private Sectors)

Company	Estimated Revenue £m	Market Share %
Hoskyns	103	33
AT&T Istel	39	12
EDS	37	12
Others	131	43
Total	310	100

Note: EDS figures exclude capital revenues.
Source: Calculated from table in Willcocks and Fitzgerald (1994, p. 154).

Competition is fierce for smaller companies, but less so for large, general vendors who can compete in all sectors. Willcocks and Fitzgerald (1994) have observed the development of a two-tier market with 'a few very large, increasingly global players offering the whole range of outsourcing services, and secondly, an increasing number of smaller, niche vendors'. If the rule of thumb is that if four companies account for more than 40 per cent of the market it is an oligopoly, the UK, as shown in Table 5.1, is oligopolistic.

Private sector companies across Europe now outsource on average around 7 per cent of their information technology operations (Willcocks and Fitzgerald, 1994, p. 10). In a survey of 160 organizations across sectors in the UK, Willcocks and Fitzgerald identified 51 per cent of UK organizations outsourcing some of their IT operations, 66 per cent outsourcing less than 20 per cent and 12 per cent outsourcing 70 per cent or more. Thus the aggregate figures conceal a wide variation in the shape of the relationship clients have with their vendor companies. These arrangements range from transactional arrangements (a type of 'spot contracting') to partnership agreements and fall into five broad categories:

Ad-hoc consultancy means bringing in private sector consultants as and when required at any stage during a computer project. The contractor supplies skilled personnel who will be managed by the client company.

Contracting out includes purchasing strategies which subject each decision to competitive tendering and includes specifying a development project which the contract company will undertake to supply by a certain deadline.

Facilities management involves a supplier taking over a specific operation or function on a long-term basis, for example a computer centre.

Systems integration has come to mean anything that involves a company 'knitting together' an alliance of software and hardware, sometimes already existent within the customer's organization and sometimes bought in from third, fourth or fifth parties.

Partnership agreements include 'preferred supplier' arrangements (sometimes called the 'Japanese model' (Willcocks and Fitzgerald 1994, p. 15)), where the client turns to a given contractor first for IT needs, as and when they arise or 'strategic alliance' arrangements where a supplier will be chosen to supply all or a subset of a client's IT needs and IT is seen as the supplier's responsibility in a partnership arrangement.

The closer relationships between vendors and clients implied by the last two categories of outsourcing arrangements are a more recent development. Systems integration has been described by some commentators as 'a market born out of computer confusion' (*Business Week*, 25 April 1988). Often it will fulfil the need of a company that has carried out prolonged and extensive outsourcing to co-ordinate the systems that they have already developed. The concept was developed after 1985, when United Airlines Inc. offered IBM $300 million to patch together United Airlines' disparate reservations computers into a more coherent hardware and software system and IBM labelled the contract 'systems integration'.

The trend away from 'spot contracting' and towards systems integration and strategic alliances and partnership arrangements has been a partial factor in the tendency for IT contracts of all kinds to increase in size and variety. The average life of an IT outsourcing contract in the UK and Europe is five to seven years; in the US they are larger, with ten years not uncommon. Systems integration is frequently described as a first step towards fuller outsourcing arrangements (Willcocks and Fitzgerald, 1994, p. 11). Systems integrators often aim to develop expertise in a wider range of their clients' 'systems' than merely developing information systems, seeing information systems as intertwined with other service functions. Some of these contracts are seen as real partnership arrangements by the participants, with an element of risk-sharing, where

> those in charge of business operations will concentrate on building alliances and partnerships which bring specific skills and solutions to support their plans … this is already moving facilities management beyond IT-centred deals to relationships with third party suppliers to provide and support specific processes. (Ronald Bain of Electronic Data Systems, *Financial Times*, 21 October 1992)

Thus a new outsourcing model is now developing – a vertical cut of business process rather than the horizontal cut of information technology. For example the Computer Sciences Corporation has entered an eleven-year agreement with British Home Stores under which it will take over the company's computing and 115 staff but also work with it to sell the combined expertise of the two organizations to the retail industry. The company Electronic Data Systems (EDS) is now signing contracts under which it will take on system development at no cost; in return it takes a percentage of the business gains by the customer. The managing director of EDS was quoted in 1993 as saying that this type of contract will account for 70 per cent of EDS' growth in the next three to five years (*Financial Times*, 21 September 1994). Thus when EDS bids for an information technology deal, the company's long-term aim will be to gain control of a wider range of functions and some measure of profit sharing.

The Core Competencies Argument

In private sector companies, radical outsourcing strategies of this kind are justified through the 'core competencies' argument. As information systems expanded in terms of expenditure as a percentage of operations and grew in complexity, companies came to realize that to carry out this function they would have to be specialists in information technology as well as in their original 'core' function. Strategic partnerships are supported by the notion of 'core competencies', developed by writers on business strategy such as Quinn:

> Each manufacturer needs to evaluate every service activity in its value chain and its staff overheads, determine if it is 'best in world' at that activity, and, if it is not, consider outsourcing the activity to the best-in-world supplier. … As it selectively outsources its less efficient activities, it may leverage its own unique resources and talents to a much greater extent. (Quinn, 1992, pp. 208–9)

Following this strategy, Nike Inc., the sports clothing 'producer', is basically a research, design and marketing organization. Quinn ascribes its compound annual growth rate to the fact that, even when number one in its market, Nike outsourced 100 per cent of its footwear production, thereby owning no production facilities and seeking to provide its greatest value at the pre-production (research and development) and post-production (marketing and sales) levels, while 'closely overseeing the quality and responsiveness of its production units'.

OUTSOURCING OF INFORMATION TECHNOLOGY IN THE UK CENTRAL GOVERNMENT

In line with private sector practice, a growing proportion of the computer systems within the UK government are maintained and developed by private sector companies. The total percentage of information technology expenditure that was outsourced in government departments in 1993 was 26 per cent, ranging from 16 per cent in the Department of Education to 61 per cent in the Department of National Heritage (Kable, 1994, p. 31). The proportion has steadily increased since 1993, with the implementation of market testing and some radical outsourcing deals in 1995. Thus government agencies are contracting out a higher percentage of information technology than private sector organizations and this percentage can be expected to continue increasing. The Department of National Heritage, outsourcing the highest percentage of its IT expenditure among government departments in 1993, provides a good indicator of the future, as it is a relatively new agency and had no previous organizational or technological 'baggage' to influence decisions over how to operate its new computer department, which was immediately contracted out (Kable, 1994).

Several pressures are currently at work on civil service managers to make contracting out the most likely option. First, shortage of skilled information technology staff has long been a problem for private and public sector companies but especially for government agencies unable to offer competitive salaries to skilled personnel. Second, the recognition that technological development introduces spiralling complexity into IT development means that specialist companies can provide attractive economies of scale and scope. Third, decisions to outsource, especially where a large percentage of operations are contracted out, are rarely reversed due to the difficulties in rebuilding technological expertise, so there is a 'ratchet' effect. These pressures are not unique to public organizations.

Other pressures to outsource come from central government initiatives: Next Steps and Market Testing. Under the Next Steps programme, governmental functions are bundled into agencies and in several instances the information technology divisions of agencies have been separated off into discrete agencies. These have then been seen as ripe for privatization under the 'Prior Options' review, when privatization must be considered as an option. Under the Market Testing programme, first proposed by the Treasury in 1991 and now being implemented throughout central government, managers are pressurized to locate areas of work suitable for contracting out. It was widely accepted from the beginning that the largest part of the Market Testing programme would be in information technology services, with IT specifically identified as a 'promising candidate' in the Market Testing guidelines (OPSS, 1993). The information technology activity in Agriculture, Customs and Excise, Defence, Employment, the Foreign Office, the Home Office, the Inland Revenue, the Lord Chancellor's Office, the Northern Ireland Office, the Office of Public Service and Science, the Department of Trade and Industry, the Department of Transport and the Welsh Office were all earmarked for Market Testing. William Waldegrave who implemented the first stages of the Market Testing as the Minister for OPSS, later specified information technology as one of the areas 'where the Government could not maintain the investment and expertise necessary to compete effectively with the private sector and from which it was best for the Government to withdraw' (Treasury and Civil Service Select Committee, 1994, p. xvii).

As in the private sector, central departments undertake a wide range of outsourcing arrangements, varying from ad hoc consultancy to privatization of information technology offices. The agencies within the Department of Social Security are the highest users of ad hoc consultancy: over 8 per cent of its IT budget in 1993 (Kable, 1994). The Benefits Agency is also a long-term user of facilities management services, having contracted out three of its four area computer centres since the mid-1980s.

Recently, there have been examples of more radical outsourcing by government agencies. In 1993, the information technology arm of the Department of Transport (the DVOIT) became the first Next Steps agency to be privatized. The Department of Transport offered the agency for sale at the price of £5.5 million, at the same time offering service contracts for information technology services worth £70 million pounds. In November 1993 the process of assimilating the agency into EDS began; its 480 staff could either become EDS employees or leave. DVOIT services the computers of the Driver and Vehicle Licensing Agency (70 per cent of DVOIT's work), the Vehicle Inspectorate, the Driving Standards Agency and the Department of Transport. DVOIT's workload was 'squeezed' (as the *Financial Times* put it) on to EDS' computers and the Swansea data centre closed. The DVOIT computers (three mainframes which can be accessed from four thousand terminals in two hundred offices throughout the UK) will be used elsewhere in the EDS group (*Financial Times*, 13 December 1993, p. 9). EDS was also successful in winning service contracts to a value of £70 million over the next five years to service DVOIT's customers.

Another example of radical outsourcing was the privatization of the Information Technology Office (ITO) of the Inland Revenue in 1993. After a competitive tendering process, Electronic Data Systems won the contract which was awarded for an initial ten years worth around £1 billion for ten years; the company have taken over the work, assets and 1900 staff of the ITO in Europe's largest data processing outsourcing deal. The contract is based on the specification of a constant volume of work, with a fixed price that goes down 50 per cent over the contract period. This is known as a fixed service charge, which year by year is fixed for ten years; if the Inland Revenue require other services then these will be charged for separately.

There is a tendency for companies successful in tendering for government contracts such as these to fall into the upper tier of the computer company market shown in Table 5.1. Some government computer systems are unique by virtue of their size and only the largest companies could contemplate handling the massive DVOIT workload, including the database and processing of details of all UK car drivers and owners. Under the European Union Transfer of Undertakings (Protection of Employment) (TUPE), the 320 DVOIT staff who eventually transferred to Electronic Data Systems from the DVOIT were entitled to retain their existing terms and conditions of employment, representing a 'major liability' (NAO, 1995b) to any purchaser. The 1900 Inland Revenue staff transferred from the Information Technology Office in the Inland Revenue deal were also covered under TUPE, representing an even greater liability. The Inland Revenue, when looking for tenders for their Information Technology Office spoke initially only to companies with more than twenty thousand staff worldwide.

This evidence that increasingly large and global players operate and develop central (and local) government information systems supports Dunleavy's (1994) argument that developments related to 'new public management' changes in government will 'clear the ground for a transformation of the commodification dynamic in public services where a few large companies are able to put a proprietorial stamp on what is being supplied'. Electronic Data Systems especially looks set to develop along the lines detailed in Dunleavy's model. Electronic Data Systems is the largest computer company in the world and ranks third in its share of the UK computer services market (see Table 5.1) with a global turnover of £5670 million and a net worth of $12 billion. EDS has long been a player in central government computing, now running two out of four of the area computer centres of the Benefits Agency and having several other contracts with government agencies including with the Ministry of Defence. EDS purchased the UK company SD-Sicon in 1991; a company which had collapsed over penalty payments on large contracts and over-trading, but with good contacts with government customers (Kable, 1994).

Thus the automation of the state has drawn new players into government. As the organizational tasks used to implement the tools of government policy have been replaced by information systems and subsequently externalized to private sector companies, information systems are acting as a funnel from public to private sector. Such a process is not easily reversible. It is widely accepted that the Inland Revenue will never operate their information systems again; the process of reconstituting the in-house organization would take at least five years and such an option is considered by the Inland Revenue to be 'very unlikely' (NAO, 1995b, p. 31). The National Audit Office report covering the sale of DVOIT makes no mention of the possibility of buying it back (NAO, 1995a).

CONTRACT MANAGEMENT: THE CORE COMPETENCY OF THE AUTOMATED STATE?

Once information technology development has been outsourced, control over information systems and the policy possibilities they present relies heavily on the contract. Even in Quinn's euphoric account of radical outsourcing, strong emphasis is placed on the importance of control structures in strategic partnerships:

> new internal structures – notably, vastly improved logistics systems, information systems that extend in depth into suppliers' operations, sophisticated technical and strategic monitoring capabilities, and improved top-level expertise to craft and manage contractual relationships in detail – become crucial. (Quinn, 1992, p. 80)

Controlling the EDS contract will now be the key activity within the Inland Revenue Information Technology Office and the Contract and Finance division of the ITO now plays a key organizational role. EDS will be allowed to communicate with the 'customers' of ITO, the other divisions and the Executive offices but any additional piece of work must be negotiated with the Contract and Finance division of ITO (otherwise it will not be paid for), a device established to ensure that ITO gets as much as possible at the basic rate. Thus the role of the Contract and Finance division becomes the crucial point in control over the inputs and outputs of EDS' work. The Inland Revenue model is likely to be adopted by other departments in the future. The Chief Executive of the Information and Technology Services Agency (ITSA) of the DSS announced in January that the bulk of ITSA's service delivery function is to be transferred to the private sector in 1995, including the transfer of around half of its staff. Thus ITSA's role will be control and regulation of whatever company wins the contract; Electronic Data Systems won 85 per cent of the contracts.

The history of government contracting suggests several warnings for the operations of such contracts (for examples see Turpin, 1972; Kelman, 1990; Fesler and Kettl, 1991: 258–61; Garvey, 1992: 37–47). First, there is the danger of asymmetry of expertise and information between the government agency and the supplier. Government overseers tend to become quickly out of line with the private sector company they are controlling. EDS employees working on the Inland Revenue contract will be highly trained specialists, while the contract management team of the Inland Revenue will be generalists. Contract management is not normally regarded as a prized position for a civil service high flyer. Currently the staff remaining in the Information Technology Office have detailed knowledge of the computer systems that EDS will manage, having worked on them over a long period of development. But over time, their expertise will date and diminish as they focus on the details of the contract. Furthermore, the amount of resources to be allocated to contract management is considerably less than a private sector company would devote to such a major contract. Around three hundred staff are left in the Inland Revenue IT office, but this number is expected to reduce over time. Private sector companies calculate that as a rough estimate, 5 per cent of a contract value should be devoted to subsequently managing the contract: in the case of the Inland Revenue/EDS partnership the percentage is around 0.4 per cent (based on figures in NAO, 1995, p. 11), which would seem to increase the risk inherent in the contract.[2]

A second common problem with government contracts is caused by the fact that they are generally run to the tightest possible profit margins, with ministers and officials tending to associate too intimate a relationship with vendors as engendering risk of fraud or corruption. This attitude draws government contract relationships away from the more relational contracting preferred in the private sector, illustrated by the following comments of the Head of the Efficiency Unit: 'We are encouraged, by some contractors, away from the concept of a classic competition, with in-house bids and outside contenders, towards the concept of strategic partnerships .... Selecting a supplier to Government because we felt comfortable with the fit could lay the Government open to the charge that business was simply being given to suppliers without a proper selection process' (Oughton, 1994, p. 9).

The Inland Revenue's strategy for dealing with EDS is fairly typical, with one official defining the role of the contract management team to 'forget all about partnership' and to make sure that 'EDS do exactly what the contract says and we are not paying them a penny more than we ought to.' This type of contract management can cause companies to displace their expertise into a search for profit surrogates (Dunleavy, 1994). Surrogates include maximizing the contract length, custom building of systems to maximize the chances of winning future contracts, regulation avoidance strategies and enlarged involvement. Companies like IBM and AT&T have long used their systems software to lock their customers into their equipment (Quinn, 1992, p. 183). A rational company pursues all these strategies to the full once the contract is awarded, staying just below penalty levels or contract cancellation levels, easing up when enlargement is possible or when contract renewal is imminent. In their contract with the Inland Revenue, EDS are prepared initially to work to very low margins, partly because the Inland Revenue has given them maximum planning visibility. The most likely profit surrogate that EDS will look for will be an extension of their role within the Inland Revenue, absorbing any function of the Inland Revenue which they can run profitably. One official observed that:

> If we were a private sector organisation this would be the first step for them and they would then be seeking to persuade us to outsource a lot of our administrative functions to them as well. Now I am not sure that they have completely given up on that. I mean I think they would quite like eventually to be running all the tax offices for example .... They know that the department will under the present government be under pressure to market test various other components of this and I am sure they will be interested in trading on from that position and being in a good position to bid for other business if it comes along.

It is worth noting that Quinn's 'core competencies' argument specifies that outsourcing partnerships should be developed only with non-competing companies. He emphasizes the importance of maintaining strategic focus:

> To maintain its position from a strategic viewpoint, the company's selected focus must control some crucial aspects of the relationship between its suppliers and the marketplace. ... And it must defend itself from big purchasers attempting to vertically integrate into its turf. (Quinn, 1992, p. 235)

Whatever the core competencies of the future Inland Revenue are likely to be, EDS' status as non-competitive will require careful monitoring, given the company's preference for contracts that contain some aspect of vertical integration.

THE FUTURE OF THE AUTOMATED STATE

As noted earlier, information technology already introduces a layer of organizational complexity for policy makers seeking to understand administrative capacity. Politicians may not be interested in bureaucracy, but most would purport to understand how it operates; the same is not true of information systems. Radical outsourcing adds another layer of complexity, increasing the number of inter-organizational boundaries between policy makers and personnel with detailed knowledge of administrative tasks. Policy advice relies on information; information about current policy problems and analysis of feedback from current operations. Policy advisers must know what information is available or could be available were computer systems modified or developed. In the case of the Inland Revenue or the customers of the DVOIT, policy advisers will rely heavily on EDS to provide information and feedback.

When policy innovations relying on technical solutions are under consideration, the role of the new actors in taxation policy making will also be central. For example, the idea that all citizens should carry a smart card containing basic information about them and their transactions with government organizations would be unworkable without a sophisticated technological solution hitherto impossible. In 1995 moves towards the introduction of a national identity card based on a fingerprint recognition system are evident; several companies are already gearing to provide the solution: EDS, running the only government fingerprint recognition system currently in existence, in Los Angeles County's welfare department, is a likely candidate. If the radical policy option of merging the tax and social security systems were to be considered, the advice on how it might be achieved would be most likely to come from EDS, currently the only organization with detailed knowledge of the information systems within the Inland Revenue and Benefits Agency. Quinn (1992, p. 78) stresses that the interface between the customer and suppliers will be where innovations in company strategy come from: 'it is well known that a high percentage – about two-thirds in the industries studied – of all innovation occurs at the customer–supplier interface'. Certainly, in order to retain control over policy advice and more crucially over policy innovation, there appears to be a need emerging for a new organizational formation within the department whose role it is to liaise with EDS, to understand their operations and to keep track of technological developments.

Radical outsourcing of the kind undertaken by the Inland Revenue is justified through the notion of core competencies and private sector companies devote considerable time and effort to developing these. The Information Technology Office of the Inland Revenue appears to have accepted its core competency as the regulation and monitoring of EDS and whatever company might tender for future contracts. The Information Technology and Services Agency of the DSS, previously identified as departmental IT regulator, IT agent (acting as IT broker, providing business analysis expertise and advice on IT matters) and IT provider (delivering IT products and services), has now outsourced the second two functions and its core function will become that of a regulator.

If the trends outlined above continue, with both government information technology contracts and the companies that compete for them increasing in size, it seems possible that major global systems integrators will become the 'East India Companies' of the future. The irreversibility of radical outsourcing decisions and the possibilities for vertical integration seem likely to put companies like EDS in a near monopoly position when the Inland Revenue or DVOIT contracts are opened for tender. In the eighteenth century, several countries including Britain subjected trade to the East Indies to an exclusive company, a development severely criticized by Adam Smith. Smith described how the British East India Company was sovereign in the East Indies, while continuing to act as a merchant in the global market: 'As sovereigns, their interest is exactly the same with that of the country which they govern. As merchants, their interest is directly opposite to that interest' (Smith, 1776, p. 499). If, with an imaginative leap, the information technology of the Inland Revenue is regarded as the East Indies, the contradictions inherent in EDS' relationship with the Inland Revenue seems reminiscent of this observation. As partners with the Inland Revenue, they have every interest in producing innovative quality systems cheaply and efficiently; as merchants, they will be driven to search for profit surrogates. If EDS do become Adam Smith's 'East India Company' of the future, with exclusive rights to the technological solutions that departments develop, Smith's damning conclusion on the activities of the East India company might be regarded as a warning for the future of the automated state:

> Such exclusive companies, therefore, are nuisances in every respect; always more or less inconvenient to the countries in which they are

established, and destructive to those which have the misfortune to fall under their government. (Smith, 1776, p. 502)

The core competency of the automated state will be to monitor, control and direct the new actors operating the new nervous system of government. The radical outsourcing deals entered into, and the particular nature of government contracts means that they have set themselves a difficult task. Agencies such as the Inland Revenue and the Benefits Agency face a dilemma that private sector companies experimenting with radical outsourcing have long recognized. Some areas of the information technology 'function' can actually be crucial to retaining core competencies and strategic capabilities in the future: what Quinn (1992) terms 'strategically essential'. Indeed, the number of 'total outsourcing' contracts that US banks are signing with companies like EDS has stopped growing and has even showed some evidence of decreasing.

The core competencies argument rests on the idea that a company (or presumably a government) should only do something if it can be 'best in world' at that activity. It would seem unlikely to many observers that government agencies should identify the development of complex information systems as something at which they could defeat the cream of the computer company or systems integration market. But it is worth noting that government agencies once led the field in producing computer systems and that the Inland Revenue computer systems have been described as the 'Rolls-Royce' of government computing. The possibility of developing existent capabilities such as that acquired over twenty years by the Inland Revenue might have provided a new vision of the core competencies of the automated state. By default, agencies such as the Information Technology Services Agency of the DSS and the Inland Revenue Information Technology Office have identified their core competencies as writing and regulating contracts. It remains to be seen whether they can be 'best in world' at writing contracts.

NOTES

1. For a useful summary of research in this area, see Snellen (1994).
2. There are forty-three risk factors identified in the National Audit Office Report (NAO, 1995b, Appendices 1 and 3).

6   Recycling or Reinventing?: The Search for Governmental Efficiency

Grant Jordan

INTRODUCTION

Reinventing is a strange word. Outside the discussion sparked off by Osborne and Gaebler, it is mainly used pejoratively to signify an ill considered or pointless activity – as in 'reinventing the wheel'. However, in Britain the reaction to Osborne and Gaebler (1992) has been to claim some pre-emptive 'glory' – not 'Me too', but 'Me first'. Sir Peter Kemp, former Project Manager for the Next Steps programme, argued, 'Osborne and Gaebler have indeed achieved a cult status, but they still appear to be well short of us where it matters, which is actually bringing about changes on the ground and reaping the benefits' (1994, p. 593). Sir Robin Butler, Cabinet Secretary and Head of the Home Civil Service, claimed that when Gaebler visited the UK in December 1992 he thought that the British had managed to plagiarize the Osborne/Gaebler agenda (1994, p. 265).

The first point in this chapter is to suggest that it is true that in Britain certain developments in the Osborne and Gaebler territory were in train, but that is because the search for efficiency is perennial: 'reinventing' is a label seeking to give special significance to what is only another episode of reform. Of which particular period is it true that there was no interest in efficiency? We are no more (or less) reinventing government than in previous cycles of reform. One can be sympathetic to the aims of reform while being sceptical about the idea that we are watching the first serious attempt: if reinvention is a sensible idea, it is not a new one. As Downs and Larkey (1986) put it:

> The same strategies, usually renamed, are tried again and again with limited success. Rarely do proponents ask why previous attempts achieved only modest success ....

Thus one reaction to the marketing of the reinvention of government is that the claims are ahistorial. Only those singularly ignorant of, or choosing to ignore, the battle against inefficiency over the years and decades can assume that the changes of the past ten years are of a scale different from past innovations – Central Policy Review Staff, Programme Analysis and Review, hiving off, corporate management, New Model Offices, cost-benefit analysis, zero-based budgeting, and so on. There is now a political premium on presenting this continuation of interest as innovation. Based on extensive interviews over a long period, Colin Campbell and Graham Wilson have observed:

> Returning to London for a set of interviews in Summer 1993, we found profound disillusionment over the directions that management reform had taken under the Major government. The political leaders had become almost evangelical in their belief that they could build-down government much further and make the surviving parts run like Marks and Spencer. (1995, p. 241)

The main developments in British central government in the past decade are the creation of Next Steps agencies (108 of them by May 1995) and market testing, but where is the convincing justification that defends the introduction? Are these developments compatible and how do they relate to that international agenda set out by Osborne and Gaebler? A slim pamphlet, *Public Service and the Future*, by William Waldegrave (1993) – discussed below – is hardly the equivalent of a Royal Commission. What we have got from government was described by one senior civil servant as 'cherrypicking'. In other words Ministers have looked selectively at possible benefits from possible changes and convinced themselves, and then tried to convince the public, that they can have these desirable features – without any adverse consequences. But as John Stewart has pointed out, in fact such changes necessarily threaten existing strengths: there is no free lunch for administrative reformers (1993, p. 8). Should the redesign of British administration not proceed on the basis of consideration of advantages and disadvantages of different options? Is the task not at least worth the effort put into President Clinton's National Performance Review in the US? Under Al Gore, 250 civil servants worked in two teams for six months to produce *From Red Tape to Results: Creating a Government that Works Better and Costs Less* (Margetts, 1994). In contrast, one of the authors in Britain of *Improving Management in Government: the Next Steps?* said that the programme was based on ninety days' study and cost £50000 (Goldsworthy, 1991). This glorifies the 'cheap and dirty' approach: garden shed (re)invention.

WHERE IS THE STARTING POINT?

In trying to discuss these developments there is a difficulty caused by the fact that we do not know the government's starting point – far less its ultimate objective. Ministers are prone to dramatically different assessments of the public sector – usually depending on the audience. Is the British civil service a problem to be solved or not? 'If it ain't broke don't fix it.' In lieu of a British rationale from those who want to transform our civil service they have taken to bestowing a retrospective justification for the changes by endorsing for Britain the arguments of Osborne and Gaebler (1992). Their book accepts as (new) gospel any assertion about waste in the US:

> waste in government does not come tied in neat packages. It is marbled throughout our bureaucracies ... it is employees on idle, working at half speed – or barely working at all .... It is the $100 billion that Bob Stone estimates that the Department of Defense wastes with its foolish overregulation. Waste in government is staggering. (1992, p. 23)

The public sector is pushed by Osborne and Gaebler to be more entrepreneurial but the private sector exemplars are ephemeral; many of the companies that even in the early 1980s looked like models have tarnished reputations. The fact that these private sector guiding lights are extinguished quite quickly stems from two factors, both of which cause problems from those who simply believe that the public sector 'should be more like the private sector'. First, some of the individuals who *appeared* most successful in the private sector have done so by perverting the market system rather than making best use of it. Second, and probably more seriously, it is a virtue of competitive capitalism that new companies thrive at the expense of the older. That means that we should expect a turnover of market leaders. This characteristic impermanence of units of the capitalist system seems difficult to reconcile with the notion of an administrative machine with a need for continuity.

Though many reformers take the need for public sector reform to be axiomatic, until the public choice critique from political economy there was remarkably little criticism from academic sources about British administration. The public administration academic community has been largely uncritical of the large, meritocratic, service – delivering civil service. There has been consistent support for the introduction of previous generations of reform – at least until their lack of impact was demonstrated. Whatever was wrong with Britain it was not, according to our public administration community, the public sector issue. They, not necessarily wrongly, saw the attack on the organization and scale of the mainstream civil service as 'scapegoating' by a Conservative government.

The usual complaint by Conservative politicians is that academics are iconoclastic and recklessly seeking to destroy what has evolved in the past. So there is a massive irony here of academics asking the government to respect trusted institutions in society and the latter seeking transformation. In January

1994 the then Chief Secretary to the Treasury, Michael Portillo, complained that:

> What's really changed is not the kind of people who hold high office so much as the attitude of the elite towards them. If we approach any office holder with sufficient malice and sufficient will to destroy, of course we can cover them with contempt and ridicule. (*Observer*, 16 January 1994)

He complained that 'cynical pessimists are eroding confidence in our institutions' (*A Week in Politics*, 15 January 1994). In fact it is the government's stock in trade (in Portillo's words) to 'belittle and undermine the fabric of our society'. As David Marquand has noted the hallmark of the Thatcher and Major governments has been, 'a ferocious, unsleeping onslaught on institutional autonomy, diversity and stability in the name of the universal rationality of the market place' (Marquand, 1994, p. 125). William Waldegrave, then Minister with responsibility for the Office of Public Service and Science, attacked people who write 'clever new constitutions' and praised the low centre of gravity of British institutions which are not 'easily pushed over by the chattering classes'. He praised the constitutional Darwinian principle which means that the traditional features of the constitution and society are not so accidental in their form as the ignorant may believe (1993a, p. 5). And yet this advocate of evolution and conservatism immediately goes on to argue for completing the Thatcherite revolution 'by reforming the public services'. In discussing health, education, the Citizen's Charter, market testing, he claims the 'radicalism of these reforms' as a virtue (1993a, p. 7). Constitutional innovation is thus a 'bad' but it appears that ill considered civil service experimentation is a 'good'.

He argued that the new structure of public service rests on five key concepts:

- separation of the purchaser of a public service from the provider of that service;
- privatization;
- Next Steps programme;
- extension of competition by market testing;
- the Citizen's Charter. (1993, p. 13)

Is the case made that the public sector required this major transformation? And that these changes actually improve on the status quo? That the changes are coherent? Or are the changes as weakly based in evidence and misguided as Waldegrave considers proposed reforms in other areas to be? The dominant academic perspective on these changes has been of scepticism. There is an assumption that the British civil service (like British higher education) was something that stood up well to international comparison. It was effective, reliable and free from corruption. These were all qualities to which other systems aspired. Reformers may be disgruntled at the lack of academic enthusiasm, but there is a limit to the number of times that the doctor can offer infallible cures for the one illness. We have had the FMI, Rayner Reviews, PAR, MINIS, Trading Funds, departmental agencies, performance pay. Since all of these developments had been declared successes by their advocates and administrators, in this perspective a civil service that was working well is potentially put at risk by ill-thought-out changes of the Next Steps and market testing type.

CHANGE AND CONSEQUENCES

There is a governmental assumption that change = improvement. In fact change = difference. The direction of change need not be improvement. Ministers and central government officials conflate scepticism about their favoured reform agenda as complacency about the issue, but in fact one might accept that public bureaucracies are poor at responding to changed environments, absorb unacceptably high proportions of resources in administration, serve the interests of staff rather than the public (and paradoxically, might provide unsatisfying and frustrating work for staff) – and still have reservations about particular reforms. It is possible to see the problems that the government have in mind – but be unconvinced about the merits of the proposed change.

Critics of the government are worried that ill-thought-out change could yield a public service that is worse than the *status quo ante*. What are identified as problems may well be solutions to past difficulties. The processes that evolved in traditional civil service systems did not do so in a perverse insistence that money be wasted, but because it was recognised that too much flexibility was dangerous. Doing away with controls opened the door to a con. It is almost an iron law of the con that it has to be grabbed immediately (before common sense gets the better of greed). Osborne and Gaebler commend an official in Visalia (California) who heard that the US Olympic committee was selling off its swimming pool. He raced to get a non-refundable deposit of $60000 'and took a check down that afternoon'. They quote an admiring school superintendent: 'Its something you'd find in private enterprise. You don't have the bureaucracy you have to deal with in most governments' (1992, p. 4). Speed and responsiveness may be desirable, but there are other factors? How is speed reconciled with political control? How can we ensure that this sort of freedom is not tempting in terms of corruption?

The erosion of controls gave freedom to Tony Williams, a civilian employee (Deputy Finance Director) in the London police, to steal over £5m (jailed in May 1995). Controls exist as deliberate features of bureaucracy and not gratuitous burdens. The fact that Williams was allowed to draw funds without supervision to finance a 'spotter' aircraft to combat the IRA shows that restrictions are an administrative necessity rather than (as well as) a nuisance. Procedures that allow no initiative are not rewarding environments in which to work, so there are benefits for staff in delayering control and minimizing regulation, but that is different from suggesting that controls are by definition useless and expensive.

Osborne and Gaebler argue, 'If it costs far more to eliminate corruption than we save by doing so, is it worth the expense?' They note that to control the 5 per cent who were dishonest, rules were created to frustrate the other 95 per cent (1992, p. 111). But it is perhaps simple minded to advocate crudely dismantling the regulatory structures. More realistically, in February 1994 Sir John Bourn of the National Audit Office argued against the prevailing contempt for 'unnecessary red tape and bureaucracy'. He was reported as saying that businessmen and others brought in to run newly created semi-autonomous agencies lacked traditional public service values and rules (*Daily Telegraph*, 2 February 1994). As O'Toole argued the 'existing' was the response to past demands:

> The evolution of a unified and career bureaucracy was a slow, at times piecemeal, process, but nevertheless it was a process accompanied by considerable thought, energy and vision on the part of those who were responsible for its development. (1989, p. 51)

Red tape may be the means to prevent unacceptable 'freelancing'. Osborne and Gaebler accept (p. 112) that every rule was originally laid down with the best of intentions, but they seem to wish to avoid the problem that these rules pose with a dramatic (and probably not feasible) leap rather than work out the difficult choice and balance involved.

Though these policies are in the name of efficiency, those on the right are well aware (in other contexts) that good intentions are not what counts. It is not necessarily the case that changes in the name of efficiency are the same as changes in efficiency. Julian le Grand (quoted in *Sunday Telegraph*, 6 March 1994) shows that any increase in performance has to be linked to increased spending rather than new management skills – 12 per cent p.a. in 1991–3 – as opposed to an average of 1 per cent growth through the 1980s. Right-wing critics of the reforms complain that the introduction in 1988 of what the then Health Minister, Kenneth Clarke, called the 'qualities of competition, choice, and measurement of quality to be found in private industry', in fact led to 'unanticipated waves of bureaucratisation' (*Sunday Telegraph*, 6 March 1994). After ten months' operation the new Child Support Agency was delivering half the target rate of benefit savings. Although £283 million was spent in start-up costs, the actual savings secured were lower than by the Child Support Unit which the CSA replaced (*Observer*, 3 April 1994). In other words, the efficiency oriented reforms need not lead inevitably to change in the desired direction.

THE PROCESS OF POLICY DEVELOPMENT

O'Toole (1989) has called for a Royal Commission on the Civil Service. Even if there are grounds for scepticism about commissions as a substitute for political argument, there is little doubt that such a process would inform the debate. If the agenda for change has not been subject to external scrutiny, has it been subject to appropriate internal critique? Chipperfield has written (1994, p. 3) that in giving good professional service a civil servant needs the following qualities:

- first, the courage to give – in Lord Armstrong's words – 'honest and impartial advice, without fear or favour, and whether the advice accords with the Minister's view or not';
- second, the imagination to foresee the consequences of policies, and to judge whether they will solve the problem to which they are addressed;
- third, the creativity to devise alternative ways of solving problems;
- fourth, the sensitivity to gauge likely reactions to one's words so as to enable dialogue and communication to continue and ideas to be understood.

Simon James (1992, p. 35) has described the critical (in two senses) role of civil servants in policy making – and how this can be confused with obstruction:

> When Chancellor Dalton (Labour) fulminated against civil servants as 'congenital snag-hunters', he was right: it is their duty to hunt out the snags before the machine is set running. Ministers who come and go are eager to make their mark, want to implement their ideas fast. Civil servants, who have to live with the consequences, need to ensure that the new policy will not stall or break down after a few months. When it comes to the crunch, ministers can and do overrule official fears, but at their

own risk, as the implementation of the community charge (Poll Tax) showed.

If we apply this ideal of the constructively sceptical civil service to the pattern of policy development on agencies and market testing it appears not to fit. As well as Ministers being short term and out to make a personal mark, we seem to have organized matters to have them advised by a succession of civil servants with the same 'can do' priority. Civil servants are seconded into the centre to help implement a programme that is already underway: in effect criticism seems to have been 'organized out' of the process as staff wish to be seen as 'achievers'. This means there has been too much emphasis on the pace of reform rather than the quality or the direction. Interviews in Whitehall by Campbell and Wilson (1995, p. 218) record that this tendency by Ministers to rely on officials who they believed were sympathetic was common. A respondent told them, 'What happens is that there are certain officials who unquestioningly do the Government's bidding ....' In such a climate Ministers lose the advantage of a critical second opinion.

If there has been internal debate it has not informed wider discussion in the public domain. Civil service scepticism comes from the retired not the serving. In *The Times* (25 February 1994), a former Head and a former Deputy Head of the Home Civil Service, Lord Bancroft and Sir John Herbecq, expressed concern about the long-term effects of the changes upon the efficiency and integrity of public administration (quoted in Drewry, 1994). Of Next Steps agencies, Chipperfield (1994, p. 11) saw 'considerable difficulties in both their underlying concept, and in possible development'. He argued – well before the Howard/Lewis debacle in 1995 on the Prison Service – against the assumption that executive work can be distanced from ministerial and political control. He concludes:

> I have grave doubts about this concept; it is too reminiscent of the old distinction between policy and administration which, in government at least, foundered on two rocks – first, that nine tenths of all policy arises out of administration, and second, that ministers are interested in what is politically important. There is, alas, no notable convergence between the politically important and policy, on the one hand, and, on the other, politically unimportant and administration .... In short, this attempt to find a middle ground between privatization and a politically accountable Department lacks the firm base in theory that would lead me to look optimistically at its chance of survival.

In his memoirs the former Permanent Secretary, Sir Antony Part, described the Next Steps document as:

> a report by three junior members of the Cabinet Office putting forward
> a superficial proposal that most executive functions should be transmuted
> into agencies with more or less unfettered freedom of action. (1990, p. 190)

Ironically the individual most closely associated with the Next Steps changes
is now also critical about the policies as implemented. Sir Peter Kemp (1993)
has argued that existing developments are:

> welcome breakthroughs but they *do not add up to a revolution.* At the
> centre, in Whitehall, old attitudes and the old guard prevail. The only heads
> that have rolled have been among the revolutionaries themselves.
> (emphasis added)

Taken along with the critical academic comment these 'insider' remarks show
that these developments can be criticized by those who share the same goals
as a Ministers.

Nigel Lawson's description of the introduction of Next Steps agencies was
decidedly cool – and suggested that the Next Steps reform did not emerge
after prolonged and detailed debate:

> I was inevitably suspicious when, towards the end of 1987, I and other
> Cabinet colleagues were informed by No 10, out of the blue, of a new
> Ibbs initiative, which apparently had Margaret's enthusiastic support ...
> the main burden of which was a recommendation that the executive
> functions of Government should be hived off into separate agencies, to
> be run like businesses by chief executives ... it was clear that Ibbs had
> not addressed either of the two principal problems involved in a change
> of this kind, however attractive the concept may have been. The first was
> the question of parliamentary accountability .... But even when this was
> solved there remained the second problem, that of maintaining effective
> control of the agencies' expenditure, in which Ibbs showed no interest
> ... a long battle ensued, resulting in a lengthy concordat negotiated by
> Peter Middleton on behalf of the Treasury and Robin Butler on behalf
> of Number 10 .... The main practical advantage I see is that by creating
> accounts, boards of directors and saleable assets, future privatization may
> prove less difficult. (1993, p. 393)

PLANNING VERSUS MARKETS

It *may* be that market testing is, as claimed by William Waldegrave above,
the logical extension of the agency approach, but there may be serious incon-
sistencies between the approaches. The agency premise was that there should

be a single customer/single client relationship between the department and the unit delivering the work. The market testing idea is that the customer should 'shop around' among competing service delivery organizations. But, for better or worse, the original rationale for Next Steps agencies did not have the latter feature. In the agency model improvement was to come about by a *planning* approach of imposing on the agencies stiffer and stiffer targets – with a turnover of chief executives if performance was judged to be inadequate.

In practice many targets are missed but chief executives remain in place. For example the *Next Steps Review*, 1993, shows that the NHS Pensions Agency was meant to clear 71 per cent of pension age estimates within six weeks of request and 99 per cent within eight weeks of request; in fact the percentages attained were only 43.8 per cent and 83.4 per cent, respectively. The Driver and Vehicle Testing Agency missed two targets by 1 per cent – and argued that this was near enough as there was sampling error to take into account. It argued that another target on driving test waiting lists was missed because there was a previous backlog of applications. Ironically the more and more detailed the targets an agency is set, the less control there is as missing one or two targets is seen as less important the more there are. Again, in 1992–3 the Insolvency Service Agency missed a series of targets:

- hold first meetings of creditors within twelve weeks in at least 80 per cent of cases (75.9 per cent achieved);
- report to creditors within nine weeks in at least 75 per cent of cases (72.1 per cent achieved);
- submit reports within ten months in at least 80 per cent of possible prosecution cases (74.1 per cent of bankruptcy and 57.1 per cent of company liquidation reports achieved);
- submit reports within in fifteen months in 80 per cent of cases identified as requiring disqualification in the public interest (33.9 per cent achieved);
- complete the administration of 24 000 cases (21,236 achieved). (*Next Steps Review*, 1993)

These 'failures' are perhaps explicable as the targets were based on 36 000 cases, but in fact the recession meant that there were over 42 500 cases to be dealt with. Though the caseload fell to 36 619, performance (as measured by the targets attained) was still defective in 1993–4. Only two of six quality targets, none of the (single) financial targets, and one of the two efficiency targets were met. One of the targets claimed as 'achieved' was 'reply within ten working days to letters from Members of Parliament delegated to the chief executive'. Since no letters were delegated the ten-day target was not onerous.

Another 'achieved' target was 'bringing proceedings for disqualification of directors of failed companies in the public interest and submit prosecution reports where there is evidence of criminality'. Since there was no measure of how many should have been initiated, one is not convinced by any figure.

The original Next Steps philosophy laid stress on *changing* chief executives when things went against target. In evidence to the Treasury and Civil Service Committee in July 1990, Peter Kemp said:

> I think that if the agencies started going wrong in a broad way as opposed to one or two cases, the remedy should not be for the core departments to interfere. What should happen is fire the people in charge, change the people in charge. (Treasury and Civil Service Committee, 1990, Q 162)

The Insolvency Service experience shows weaknesses in such mechanistic arguments. The 1994 *Next Steps Review* (p. 52) says of the fall in Insolvency Service productivity in 1993–4, 'Productivity reduced by 5.9 per cent, as The Service concentrated on maintaining case administration standards.' But who should decide this priority? Managers or Ministers? And before or after the performance?

FROM NEXT STEPS TO MARKET TESTING: INCREASING THE PACE OR CHANGING DIRECTION?

It is not the existence of market testing that is new but the idea that it should be applied widely. Consideration of performing work by choosing between departmental and contractor delivery has happened in the past. In the early 1990s a programme of investigations was running at about £20 million per year. The Market Testing Initiative comes from the White Paper *Competing For Quality* in November 1991 (Cm 1730). This set a target of market testing activities worth around £1.5 bn and involving 44 000 staff in an eighteen-month period from 1 April 1992 to 30 September 1993. Provisional figures at the end of September 1993 showed that under £700m worth of activities had been reviewed. Before the Treasury and Civil Service Committee, Sir Robin Butler argued that the failure to meet targets was not serious as they were meant to be 'challenging' – so it was no bad thing if they were missed:

> Unless you set overambitious targets you don't get people to achieve more than they think they can achieve .... All targets should be difficult for people to achieve and one would not expect every target to be achieved because if one did it would not be a target which was challenging.

He argued that it was better for Next Steps agencies to attain 75 per cent of their targets than 100 per cent, as in the latter case the targets (by definition) would have been too easy. This was not the expectation on which Next Steps agencies were built. Then we were led to believe that managers would 'live or die' by their success in attaining targets.

By the end of 1993 much more of the *so called* market testing programme had been completed. Departments won two-thirds of the market tests – but the remarkable development was that only £200m worth of the programme actually went to market testing. Most of it was let as commercial contracts – *without the in-house staff being given the opportunity to compete*. Again policy was cavalierly made up as they went along. A Market Testing Bulletin (9 January 1995) produced by the Efficiency Unit claimed that over £2 bn worth of government services 'have now been reviewed since April 1992'. This form of words accurately, but economically, does not claim that this programme was market tested. By value 31 per cent of the programme was market tested (£634m). In-house teams were awarded 73 per cent of this. £1.18bn of work was awarded to outside suppliers. Of this £1bn was the result of a 'strategic decision' to contract out without an in-house bid. David Hunt (Chancellor of the Duchy) was quoted as saying, 'Once again, the United Kingdom is leading the world in reinventing the processes of government ....'

Part of the reason for this failure to meet the programme without 'strategic decisions' to guarantee private sector 'wins' can be put down to the fact that, in Peter Kemp's words, 'the turkeys have been allowed to organise Christmas' or 'The guards are in charge of the escape committee' (1993, p. 9). In other words, there is no incentive for the staff to be particularly keen to reduce their own prospects and job security in market testing experiments, and for that reason the government sought to by-pass staff who might drag their feet on change or, even worse, win the contest. In the National Performance Review in the US there is an emphasis on securing staff co-operation: this seems to be lacking in the UK.

Competing For Quality was produced within the Treasury and this source may be significant: there are at the very minimum some tensions between the market testing approach and the Next Steps developments. In the Preface to *Competing For Quality*, the then Chancellor, Norman Lamont, argued that the initiative stemmed from the Citizen's Charter. Though the connection between Next Steps and the Citizen's Charter were asserted, to those outside the centre of government the links between Next Steps, the Charter approach and market testing are not clear – below a very general level of assertion that they are designed to introduce efficiency. Do they support or contradict each other? By May 1995 the *Competing For Quality* initiative was itself the subject of a review along the lines of an efficiency scrutiny. Unusually the proposed study involved the use of surveys and group discussions to establish the views of the staff affected by the competition programme.

In an earlier Working Paper (Jordan, 1992) the central complaint about Next Steps agencies was that there was such an underdeveloped argument in their justification. There was simply an assertion that the agencies represented the extension of the earlier Financial Management Initiative. The 1992 Working Paper argued:

> Reorganization on such a scale deserves far more opportunity to consider the difficulty of planned change and to draw lessons from the past. Instead of implementation after reflection we have seen an aggressive marketing of the merits of the changes by the civil servants involved that has failed to connect this exercise with the difficulties experienced in the past.

To read the Next Steps government literature is to enter a doubt-free zone.

One does not need to read far below the surface of the semi-official history of the creation of the agencies by Goldsworthy to discover an admission that the thesis of the report was really an assertion rather than an argued case:

> Its persuasiveness lay not in the presentation of detailed evidence but in its description of a state of affairs which many readers said they recognised readily from their own experience; and in an analysis with which most of them instinctively agreed. (1991, p. 8)

This is to admit that acceptance of the benefits of change has had to be an article of faith. Goldsworthy claimed that:

> although the Government was firmly committed to implementing Next Steps, the policy itself was not publicly set down anywhere in any detail. Indeed Sir Robin Ibbs' Report had described an ideal, and sketched out – but no more – how it might be put into effect, so the policy had to be developed in the light of progress. (1991, p. 34)

It is only marginally unfair to translate this as 'we made it up as we went along'. That said, it is surely neither unexpected nor unwarranted for there to be criticisms from those looking for a coherent rationale. In 1994 there seems a similar failure of linkage in the 'story' we are told about the relationship between market testing and agencies. There is a similar underargued drift from market testing to direct contracting out.

Richards and Rodrigues (1993) note that the creation of Executive Agencies and many other changes of the 1970s and 1980s were based on the belief that the public sector could be better managed, but they query how this fits in with the move to market testing:

> After all of this effort, why the change of tack? Why the application of a ... strategy previously only used systematically to force management change in local government, which, of course, is not directly subject to central government control? *Does this mean that leading stakeholders are disillusioned with the achievements of their ... (previous) strategy, even though the public presentation of achievements is laudatory?* (emphasis added)

That Next Steps and the market testing ideas were controversial within Whitehall is signalled by the fact that Sir Peter Kemp was eased out of Whitehall in 1992. An interview with the *Independent* quoted Sir Peter as arguing that the civil service was subject to competition by 'wayward barons':

> unhappy, unsure of itself and becoming 'littered with policies that do not work'. The controversial market testing programme – the review process that can lead to contracting out – had, he claimed, gone 'hopelessly awry'.

Richards and Rodrigues say that the 'hero' of Next Steps (that is, Sir Peter Kemp) was 'thrown out on his ear'. They asked, 'Why has there been such a sharp change in direction: the Agency initiative ... seems in danger of being derailed by market testing, providing solutions from the private sector to achieve improvement.' They complain that there is no 'reasoned critique' that explains why the management reforms of the Next Steps agencies have been overtaken by the fundamentally different market testing idea.

They suggest there are two basic public service reform strategies, planning and markets. Market testing can be seen as the *reversal* of a series of management reforms (including Next Steps) that have previously been based on a design of centralized planning (1993, p. 33). They say that from 1979 the Conservative governments backed tactics to enhance the role of management: the new imposition of market testing would *replace* one reform of strategy with another. Richards (1993, p. 3) says that agencies may have proved too weak a lever of change: real contracts, enforceable in law and with no question of a hierarchical relationship between the two parties, will be much more difficult to fudge. In this light the 'agency' solution was not working.

In terms of meeting targets, the 1993 Review shows that overall only 77 per cent of targets were met in 1992/3 and that the performance in efficiency and throughput targets actually fell in the year compared to previous performance (1993, p. 9). So it may be that there should be debate as to whether agencies are the best way forward or whether a new market testing approach is preferable, but Ministers deny that there is a subject to discuss and argue that all is coherence and complementary change. As Richards and Rodrigues say,

> Whitehall does not let ordinary citizens in on its family arguments, so we have to deduce what we can from the evidence available if we want to understand these events ... in the absence of more open government the old art of Kremlinology comes in useful. (1993, p. 33)

They argue that agency chief executives resent the effort involved in market testing because they see it as a diversion from the real problems, which are to do with the reluctance to decentralize control of the detail of policy implementation manifested in the core departments and the Treasury. The 1993 Price Waterhouse report on executive agencies noted:

> some Chief Executives have been disappointed to find that their independence is considerably constrained, particularly when a Government-wide initiative like market testing affects them so fundamentally .... In addition, even though agencies have delegated powers, over pay for example, this does not preclude Treasury interference. (quoted in Campbell, 1994, p. 33)

Campbell (1994, p. 30) argues:

> I interviewed several individuals in summer 1993 who either served as chief executives of Next Steps agencies or shouldered departmental responsibility for the policies they administered. This sense of disillusionment had become very pronounced indeed. Much of this stemmed from a belief that the additional managerial initiatives – especially the Citizen's Charter and market testing – had impinged on the discretions originally imparted to chief executives ... frustrations also focused on the OPSS and Treasury three-year reviews ....

Mellon's work shows that the real level of managerial freedom in agencies may be superficial:

> the Agency initiative adopts a veneer of 'market speak' which the outsider chief executives find far from the reality of the markets that they actually faced when they worked in the private sector ... these chief executives find themselves blocked and second guessed at every turn. (1993, p. 30)

The 'Kemp' assumption was that the chief executives sorted out inefficiency in the areas covered by the agencies. If one believes that is a credible approach then it is inconsistent to also seek to bring about improvement by market testing. Quite apart from the fact that if one believes in agencies then (by definition) the problem has been solved, there is the risk that the market testing destroys the organizational morale that the chief executive is building.

Richards and Rodrigues argue that one explanation for this new direction might be the needs for the adviser on Efficiency and Effectiveness, Sir Peter Levene, and his (then) Minister, William Waldegrave, to be indulging in 'career opportunism' as they impose change to maintain (or create) 'can-do' reputations. If the reason has more respectability, it is not obvious.

The tension in these programmes is not simply about Next Steps versus market testing. After all, the Next Steps advocates seem frustrated that their freedom is so heavily restricted. There are clearly many in the civil service who are not committed to *any radical* reform at all. They would argue that increases in efficiency were being achieved by normal incremental developments. Market testing has some appeal to these institutional conservatives who argue that there is little to fear from demonstrating efficiency by going through the routines of comparison, but market testing principally appeals to those who wish to *outflank* the Next Steps programme in radicalness and who see a major shift in the pattern of service delivery as the (still) inefficient public sector is opened up to competition. In connection with the regulation of privatized utilities Burton has drawn attention to the difference between the 'competitive order' sought by the 'purist' adherents of Austrian economics and the (inadequate) 'ordered competition' (Hayek, 1948) that results from state regulation by the RPI-X model and the encouragement of duopoly in telecommunications rather than free and open competition. Burton quotes the argument of Stephen Littlechild (1986, p. 12):

> Neo-classical 'mainstream' economics tends to see the economic problem facing society as one of efficiently allocating resources in the light of preferences, techniques and resource availabilities, knowledge of which is supposed somehow to be given. Austrian economics, by contrast, sees the problem as including the *discovery* of these preferences, techniques, and resource availabilities …. (quoted in Burton, 1995)

IS THE TREASURY IN STEP?

Signals that there is Whitehall disagreement include the comments by Nigel Lawson in *The View From Number 11* (1993, p. 390). He starts his discussion with the heading 'Stumbles on "Next Steps"'. He recounts how in the first years in Office the Thatcher governments had reduced civil service staffing by 20 per cent and in 1982 created the FMI. Lawson describes how when Robin Ibbs took over the Efficiency Unit in 1983 a split emerged between the Unit and the Treasury. Lawson argued that as long as public services existed, insulated from the marketplace, Treasury control was needed. He argued that as there was no price mechanism at work, there had to be Treasury discipline or none at all. That he argued that the chaotic consequences of the collapse of the Soviet Union showed what happened when market disciplines did not replace a command system, shows the degree of opposition.

Given the Treasury suspicion of Next Steps in the Lawson era it is therefore perhaps significant that *Competing For Quality* was a Treasury document. It can be seen as the Treasury's *alternative* to Next Steps. While Lamont gave the genesis as the Citizen's Charter, it is more realistic to trace it back to the Treasury lead exercise that culminated in *Using Private Enterprise in Government: a Report of a Multi-Departmental Review of Competition, Tendering and Contracting for Services in Government Departments* (HM Treasury, 1986), which argued that:

> Competition should be a regular part of every Department's efficiency drive …. Departments should review all their activities to see if they offer scope for contracting out.

Lamont indicated that *Competing For Quality* was based on the assumption that public sector managers could buy from the public or private sector in the pursuit of quality. The government,

> had no dogmatic preference for either one over the other. We believe that the best in the public services can match anything achieved in the private sector.

This appears to signal a judiciously balanced approach by government to the matter of public or private service. But of course if one works in the public sector this was not perhaps what one hopes for from one's employer; it was as comforting as hearing from one's doctor that he was absolutely neutral on the position of whether one's leg was to be saved or amputated. For Lamont to go to say that: 'we believe that public sector managers and staff will welcome the opportunity to compare the services that they provide in fair and open competition with the best of the private sector', must be a joke. Who would seriously believe that these moves would be welcomed by staff, thirsting to give of their best in a more competitive environment? There is no proof that private sector companies *enjoy* competition: much effort goes towards its reduction. It may be that working in the private sector *is* more rewarding in a psychological and material sense, but it is surely unacceptable for an employer to pretend that casting the cloud of unemployment (or deterioration in wages or conditions) over staff with families and mortgages is good for staff morale. *Competing For Quality* said that competition would bring 'new benefits to all those who use or work in public services'. Perhaps unemployment benefit was one that the authors had in mind?

Competing For Quality stated that hitherto market testing procedures had been cumbersome because, 'the procedure has often involved a prolonged exercise to bring the in-house operation to maximum efficiency before competitive tendering can begin. After a decade of efficiency reforms there should no longer be a need to delay in this way.' Of course if there was a real confidence in the benefits of the efficiency reform, then there would be no wave of market testing.

If there is a turf battle going on between defenders of the agency approach and market testers, the tide of battle appears in favour of the latter. A committee chaired by the PM decided that Next Step agencies should not expand their activities to compete with private sector organizations. In the view of some of those in the public sector this policy is a defence of the private sector from competition. The *Independent* has noted:

> The Government wants civil servants to be entrepreneurial and competitive, but not to become carried away with money-spinning ideas. Yes, they may battle with the private sector to continue keeping the records of vehicle licences. But, no, they will not be allowed to diversify into repairing cars. State provision should be market tested, but existing private provision is not to be state-tested (23 March 1994).

In March 1994 Stephen Dorrell, then Financial Secretary to the Treasury, stated that as agency directors were frustrated by these strict Whitehall rules on their 'businesses', the agencies would be allowed to move into the private sector:

> As agencies develop their specialisms, they will be tempted increasingly to ask why they should continue to live with the undoubted constraints that they are employed by public sector ownership.

This vision of the future of the agencies sees them as moving into the private sector through privatization. This was not the original Next Steps 'game plan' but as we have seen above it was always a Treasury preference (see quotation from Lawson, above).

DIFFERENT STORIES FOR DIFFERENT AUDIENCES

There are two scripts from Ministers and market testing advocates. On the one hand the message is that what is in mind is a 'quality check' to allow civil servants the chance to show off improvements. William Waldegrave suggests that:

> although the White Paper sets clear targets for the amount of government activity which is to be market tested, there are no targets for the amount which is to be contracted out ... so there is not some sort of hidden agenda – privatization by the back door. This is first and foremost a management reform ....

But in the same speech at a conference of businessmen, he concluded:

> I hope you will be encouraged by our willingness to make it easier for the private sector to compete in these areas and that you will be sufficiently excited by the scope and scale of the new business opportunities that we are creating, to take up our challenge. (CDL speech, 18 January 1993)

The government seems ambivalent as to whether it really wants to offer work out with the Departments. Are private businesses only being used as a cheap (from the government's point of view) way to drive costs down *within* government or is there a real expectation that outside firms will become involved? The issue of Transfer of Undertakings (Public Employment) Regulations, 1981, obscures matters. This derives from an EC Directive in 1979 on 'Acquired Rights' and broadly stated that if an ongoing entity is transferred to another owner then the new owner is obliged to maintain the rights, terms and conditions of staff. This major externally driven uncertainty adds to the self-induced confusion of seeking incompatible goals.

ARE CONTRACTS THE RIGHT APPROACH?

To date the reservations about the market testing approach have concerned the practicality of the implementation. John Stewart (1993) allows there are strong arguments in favour of government by contract, but what is not convincing is that 'contacts are the appropriate form of organizational control in the public sector in all conditions and for all services' (1993, p. 9). In other words, there may be circumstances where markets and contracts 'fit' but that is not to say that they fit everywhere – or that they do not bundle up advantages and disadvantages. Stewart and Walsh (1992, p. 513) say: 'The need is to distinguish circumstances in which government by contract is appropriate, but not to assume its universal application.'

Parker and Hartley (1990, p. 9) set out relevant arguments for and against contracting out that can be applied to market testing.

The arguments for are:

- private firms in competitive markets are better managed, more innovative and more responsive to customer requirements;
- private firms are threatened with bankruptcy;
- regular recontracting means that a contractor and service levels can be reviewed;
- result is efficiency gains and cost saving.

The arguments against are:

- Poor quality, unreliable service – for example, dirty streets, schools and hospitals;
- private industry is monopolistic and not competitive;
- hidden costs of contractors – for example, organizing and evaluating bids and monitoring contracts;
- equity – the poorly paid lose out.

They stress the need to ensure the creation and maintenance of contestable markets – with obvious dangers of cartels and collusive tendering. They also noted that pressures need to be put on in-house units otherwise they will bid low to eliminate rivals with increases coming later (1990, p. 15). While the notion of savings from testing implies some kind of market in future years there may not be suitable organizations to bid for services. There is a problem over the nature of the competition once the in-house capacity has gone. This might mean that the external bidder can recognize an effective monopoly and increase prices. If the competition works to drive the unsuccessful companies out of business, there might be a lack of credible bidders in future rounds. Such competition is *generally* good for the consumer but in the provision of public services we might want to ensure capacity to deliver: we might want to put a premium for reliability over economy.

The political attraction of market testing seems to be that it offers the chance to avoid politically difficult choices. It says to those concerned about the expanded state, 'Look this will cost you less.' It says to those who value the services that it is 'business as before delivered through new (cheaper) mechanisms'. However, the problem with market testing may be that its apparent cost savings wreck the public sector pattern that has been effective, reliable and honest. Perhaps we cannot just have the old system with some savings: once we embark on looking for economies in this way then the old system, merits and defects, is altered. As Burton (1995) says about the regulation of utilities, 'The essential problem with this system of ordered competition is that it is a halfway house between government direction and the competitive order. Some may see nothing wrong in that, as such; considered more fundamentally, however, it involves the attempt to combine two quite differently-founded types of economic order.'

It might be argued that the conflict discussed here is an invention by outsiders. It was for this reason that the speech to the Conservative Reform Group in October 1993 at the Conservative Party Conference by the Foreign Secretary, Douglas Hurd, was so important:

> [W]e must show that we value those we rely upon to provide the service. The teacher, the nurse, the serviceman, the doctor, the postmaster, the police officer, the civil servant, are not relics ... whom we should periodically despatch to the rice fields for thought reform and indoctrination, are not entitled to special privileges or immunity from sacrifices, for example on pay. But they, and those whom they serve, rightly distrust any whiff of dogma which they may detect in the way governments tackle the problems of their profession.

He said that he was against the impression that the Conservative Party believed in a:

> permanent cultural revolution in the style of Trotsky or chairman Mao .... We must show that we are not driven by ideology to question every function of the state, to make impossible the life of our public servants, or to depreciate the worth and quality of the different public services. (*Independent*, 8 October 1993)

Does this sound like the endorsement of a considered and coherent reform programme, or a warning that the changes do not even convince all senior Ministers? Concern at the way things are being done is thus no longer restricted to outside academics. Sir Peter Kemp, now 'on the substitutes' bench', notes:

> [F]ew governments can resist using their control over the civil service as a means of pursuing some policies .... These often reflect the transient political concerns of the day and may have little or no bearing on the overall effectiveness of departments or agencies. Indeed they may serve to undermine it. Current and recent flavours of the month include equal opportunities, deregulation, purchasing preferences, relocation, market testing and pay policy .... However, these policies should be pursued with more care than is presently the case. (1993, p. 25)

THE COMPETITIVE RELATIONSHIP BETWEEN VALUED GOALS

In the pursuit of reform there are many wholly desirable objectives: the real world difficulty is that they are not compatible. For example, it is economically attractive to save costs by reducing core staffs and recruiting temporary staff to cover peak flows of work (what has been called 'Government by Kelly Girl'), but that runs against other goals. There is talk of 'empowering' staff, but a tendency to short-term employment is scarcely good for morale. The IRS in the US has used temporary staff to assist with queries in connection with self-assessed tax returns. But the level of error in the advice has been claimed to be as high as 85 per cent. So the 'cheap' temporary staff may be at odds with the idea of a well trained and effective staff. Sir Peter Kemp is one who has accepted that the market testing approach has degenerated into a cost-saving jobs-purge rather than a means to allow staff to release their potential.

Osborne and Gaebler concede that the traditional bureaucratic model provided certain desirable features – security, stability, reliability, fairness and equity. They say during times of intense crisis – the Depression and two world wars – the bureaucratic model 'worked superbly' (1992, p. 14). They then try to argue that in a new environment bureaucratic institutions – public and private – fail us. Another conclusion might be that we want, legitimately, the advantages of different kinds of organizations and processes. Osborne and Gaebler over-simplify by suggesting that administrative history is junk: arguably the historical outcomes were responses to need. There are examples in British local government of entrepreneurial activity which has gone wrong, for example the Western Isles Council and the money lost with BCCI, the creative currency deals of Hammersmith. Osborne and Gaebler observe that 'entrepreneurs are people who fail many times'. They write of 'Creating Permission to Fail' but within five pages are discussing replacing managers whose performance fails: so much for permission to fail. The design of government involves choosing between different packages of costs and benefits. If one chooses to remedy a specific defect one has to face up to the adverse consequences in other areas. The trouble about the real world is that it involves trade-offs among desirable goals: we want services that are cheap to deliver but with high standards; we want organizations lean but reliable; we want them flexible but predictable; we want low salaries but well motivated staff.

Campbell (1994) argues that, unlike in New Zealand, there is no coherent theory underpinning British change. His interviews uncovered comments such as:

> So, it's not all clear what's the intellectual and theoretical basis for what's being done. Moreover ... we've actually got a whole series of things mixed up together and presented as though they are a single whole ....

The reception given to Osborne and Gaebler no doubt indicates a wish to achieve better organizations rather than recognition of a means to better them. As Kay writes of business strategy,

> Too much of what is offered as strategy consists of a list of platitudes. The value of these is not negligible. Platitudes are often ... necessary assertions of important truths ... [but] the quack who promises relief often receives a warmer welcome than the practitioner who recognises the limitations of his own knowledge. (1993, p. 362)

Britain is not working to implement the Osborne and Gaebler vision: that is because *Reinventing Government* is not the guidebook to change that it appears to be. Instead it is a viewbook of attractive pictures of changes that have gone right: it does not tell us why they succeed. In Britain we are seeking desirable goals that may be inherently mutually exclusive. In particular, in shifting fashion from agencies to market testing, there is a fundamental change involved.

7 The Bureau-shaping Model and the Public Service

Stephen Cope

According to Rhodes, rational choice 'is now an established part of political science' (1991, p. 545). However, within the field of public administration he observed 'only a handful of studies drawing on this theoretical approach' (1991, p. 547), and argued 'its potential remains to be realised' (1995, p. 122). This chapter seeks to add to this collection by examining a rational choice model of bureaucratic behaviour. It evaluates the bureau-shaping model as a way of understanding key public service developments. The bureau-shaping model is essentially a reconstructed rational choice model of bureaucratic behaviour, offering potentially valuable insights into the behaviour of bureaucrats in liberal democratic states (Dunleavy, 1985; 1991, pp. 145–248). However, Dunleavy acknowledged that the model 'remains to be systematically proved' (1991, p. 247), despite claiming that it 'seems to fit closely with a large but disorganized stockpile of anecdotal data about how bureaucrats see themselves and about what they say they are trying to achieve' (1985, p. 324).

There have been a few tentative applications of the bureau-shaping model. For example, the model has been used to survey the 'architecture of the British central state' (Dunleavy, 1989a; 1989b). The model has been further applied to explain the reorganization of central government resulting from the Next Steps programme (James, 1994; 1995a; 1995b). It has also been used to examine the organization of local authorities (Biggs and Dunleavy, 1995a; 1995b), cutback management in local government (Cope, 1994), and contracting-out in local government (Cope, 1995). However, it is still too early to provide a comprehensive and systematic evaluation of the bureau-shaping model, though this chapter provides a preliminary assessment. Nevertheless, many writers acknowledged the potential of the bureau-shaping model. Dunsire argued the model is 'a great advance ... and will form part of the armoury of any future analysts of bureaucratic structure' (1995, p. 24). The bureau-shaping model is still being developed theoretically and applied empirically. Following Dowding, it is 'rather premature' to attempt to evaluate the explanatory power of the bureau-shaping model (1995, p. 91).

The chapter is organized into four substantive sections. The first section charts the origins of the bureau-shaping model by examining its theoretical antecedents – that is, rational choice theory generally and the budget-maximizing model specifically. The second section outlines the bureau-shaping model. The third section applies the model by examining its application in explaining three major developments affecting British government – namely, cutback management in local government, the Next Steps programme within central government, and the role of the European Commission in the European Union (EU). The fourth section assesses the strengths and weaknesses of the bureau-shaping model as a way of explaining bureaucratic behaviour within public service organizations.

FROM BUDGET-MAXIMIZING TO BUREAU-SHAPING

Rational choice theory provides potentially useful ways in which researchers can model the behaviour of state bureaucrats. Rational choice 'builds its models from simple assumptions about maximizing behaviour' (Dowding, 1994, p. 110). As a deductive model, rational choice theory 'proceeds from assumptions or axioms about human motives and behavior, and draws the logical institutional and policy implications from those axioms' (Almond, 1991, p. 38). Rational choice theorists assume that 'all phenomena are reducible to individual behaviour' (King, 1987, p. 94), arguing that collective entities, such as bureaucracies, can be explained only by examining the behaviour of their constitutive individuals. Furthermore, they assume that 'individuals are egotistic, utility-maximising, rational self-interested actors' (King, 1987, p. 92), tending to assume that individual motivation is generally 'hard-edged' (that is, driven by material gain) while admitting that the concept of self-interest is 'potentially extremely elastic' (Ward, 1995, p. 79). Rational choice models are thus built on the twin assumptions of methodological individualism and self-interested maximizing behaviour (Almond, 1991, p. 38; Dowding, 1991, pp. 17–29; Dunleavy, 1991, p. 3; Coleman and Fararo, 1992, pp. ix–xii; Lane, 1993, p. 155). Rational choice theory 'is not intrinsically tied to right-wing political values' (Dunleavy, 1991, p. 5). There is nothing inherently right-wing in rational choice theory, because assuming individuals are self-interested does not equate to believing, like the New Right, that the market is superior to the state. This mistaken view that rational choice is right-wing may partly explain why it has been 'greeted with indifference bordering on hostility' (Rhodes, 1995, p. 122). Following Ward:

> Applications of rational choice theory are parasitic on a range of theories for assumptions about social structure and institutional variables, and for the fleshing out of what self-interest means .... It is best regarded [as] a

set of techniques that can be appropriated by other paradigms so long as they take individual action seriously. (1995, p. 78)

Indeed, rational choice theory can be married to other theories providing its assumptions of methodological individualism and self-interested maximizing behaviour remain intact (Green and Shapiro, 1994, pp. 203–4) – for example, there is a growing body of work on rational choice Marxism (Carver and Thomas, 1995). The bureau-shaping model is a rational choice model of bureaucratic behaviour, and, moreover, an institutional rational choice model attempting to explain the behaviour of bureaucrats within institutions. It 'assumes that individual actors pursue their self-interests in an institutional environment which determines the incentives and constraints which they face' (James, 1995, p. 616). The bureau-shaping model developed as a critique of another rational choice model of bureaucratic behaviour, the budget-maximizing model.

The Budget-maximizing Model Examined

The budget-maximizing model has been developed largely through the work of Niskanen (1971; 1973; 1975; 1978; 1991). The budget-maximizing thesis represents a public choice critique of the Weberian view of bureaucracy, in which bureaucrats are assumed to execute policy made by ruling politicians (Niskanen, 1973, p. 3). Bureaucrats do not serve politicians, but instead serve themselves. This view enjoys considerable populist and intuitive appeal because it fits with 'an important everyday image of government officials' (Dunleavy, 1991, p. 200).

A bureaucrat, according to Niskanen, is 'the senior official of any bureau with a separate identifiable budget' (1973, p. 11). He argued 'a bureaucrat, like anyone else, maximises his personal utility' (1973, p. 20). Bureaucrats do not pursue some notion of public interest as, say, defined by politicians; instead they pursue their self-interests. Niskanen assumed:

> Among the several variables that may enter the bureaucrat's motives are: salary, perquisites of the office, public reputation, power, patronage, output of the bureau, ease of making changes, and ease of managing the bureau. All except the last two are a positive function of the total budget of the bureau during the bureaucrat's tenure. (1973, p. 22)

Given the reputed motivations of bureaucrats, Niskanen concluded that the utility of bureaucrats 'need not be strongly dependent on every one of the variables which increase with the budget, but it must be positively and continuously associated with its size' (1973, p. 23). Bureaucrats, in maximizing their utility, seek to maximize the budget of their bureau. However, Niskanen later argued bureaucrats 'maximize their bureau's discretionary budget, defined as the difference between the total budget and the minimum cost of producing the output expected by the political authorities' (1991, p. 18).

This disposition to maximize budgets does not mean necessarily that budgets are maximized. Niskanen argued that budget-maximization is achieved because a bureau is a monopoly producer of goods and services demanded by a sponsor (for example, government minister, legislative committee). Niskanen described the relationship between a bureau and its sponsor as a 'bilateral monopoly', because the 'bureau "sells" its service only to the government, and the government "buys" the service only from the bureau' (1975, p. 618). He noted:

> A bureau offers a promised set of activities and the expected output(s) of these activities for a budget. The primary difference between the exchange relation of a bureau and that of a market organisation is that a bureau offers a total output in exchange for a budget, whereas a market organisation offers units of output at a price …. The primary reason for the differential bargaining power of a monopoly bureau is the sponsor's lack of a significant alternative and its willingness to forego the services supplied by the bureau. (1973, p. 14)

Niskanen assumed 'a passive sponsor which knows what budget it is prepared to grant for a given quantity of services but does not have the incentive or the opportunity to obtain information on the minimum budget necessary to supply it' (1973, p. 17). If there are no other suppliers of goods and services that the sponsor requires, the sponsor is thus dependent upon a bureau for supply. The bureau, then, offers 'proposed expenditure programmes on an either-or, all-or-nothing, take-it-or-leave-it basis' (Niskanen, 1973, p. 31). Niskanen argued that a bureaucrat 'will know much more about the costs and production processes of the bureau's services than will the officers of the sponsor' (1973, p. 16). A bureaucrat collects information and distorts its presentation to the sponsor in such a way as to increase the likelihood that the sponsor approves his or her proposed budget. The sponsor lacks information to scrutinize effectively the proposed budget of a bureau to supply the required goods and services.

Furthermore, the sponsor is often sympathetic to the budgetary demands of a bureau, and thus not inclined to curb its demands. This sponsor sympathy, as Heclo observed in American government, is part of the 'glue' in forming both 'iron triangles' that tie together 'executive bureaus, interest groups, and congressional committees in all-powerful alliances' and 'issue networks' that 'comprise a large number of participants with quite variable degrees of mutual commitment or of dependence on others in their environment' (1978, pp. 100–2). Niskanen stated:

> The detailed review of a bureau's proposed budget is usually performed by a specialised committee within the government and/or legislature that is dominated by representatives of groups in the population with relatively high demands for the bureau's service (e.g. high-risk patients) or who own factors used by the bureau (e.g. a trade union of teachers) …. As a rule, the interests of the review group are served by forwarding the bureau's proposal, with minor modifications, for approval by the legislature. (1973, p. 32)

The budget-maximization thesis, therefore, assumes that a self-interested bureaucrat, whose bureau enjoys a monopoly of supplying goods and services demanded by a weak (and often sympathetic) sponsor, results in bureaucratic 'over-supply' of goods and services provided by government (Niskanen, 1978, p. 165). Niskanen maintained that 'bureaucrats maximise the total budget of their bureau during their tenure, subject to the constraint that the budget must be equal to or larger than the minimum total costs of supplying the output expected by the sponsor' (1973, p. 27). Consequently budget-maximizing behaviour of bureaucrats results in government budgets being 'too large' (Niskanen, 1975, p. 630). Niskanen claimed:

> All bureaus are too large. For given demand and cost conditions, both the budget and output of a monopoly bureau may be up to twice that of a competitive industry facing the same conditions. (1973, p. 33)

According to Dunleavy, the budget-maximization model 'has rarely been subjected to critical attention or systematic empirical testing' (1991, p. 210). This claim is perhaps a little stretched because there have been several studies of budget-maximizing (for example, see McGuire, 1981; Hood et al., 1984; Sigelman, 1986; Blore, 1987; Dunsire and Hood, 1989, pp. 87–111; Blais and Dion, 1991; Dunsire, 1991). Dunsire and Hood compared and tested models based on notions of a 'Weberian' bureaucrat, whose aim is to serve his or her political sponsors, and an 'Adam Smith' bureaucrat, whose aim is to serve himself or herself (1989, pp. 87–111). The 'Adam Smith' bureaucrat, though more than a simple budget-maximizer, pursues budget-maximizing as well as other strategies.

Most studies of budget-maximizing, however, have been conducted within an American context, by researchers ideologically attracted to New Right prescriptions, and without systematic comparison with other models. First, Peters demonstrated that European bureaucracies are different to American bureaucracies, upon which Niskanen based his model. He noted that Niskanen's budget-maximizing thesis is 'peculiarly American' (1991, p. 305), thus arguably representing more of an inductive model describing American bureaucracy than a deductive model of bureaucracy. Second, rational choice models are not inherently right-wing, and thus their normative claims need to be stripped from their theoretical claims in their appraisal as explanatory models. Consequently if bureaucrats do budget-maximize, then it does not necessarily follow that governments should be privatized because budget-maximizing strategies may be countered by restructuring relations between bureaucrats and their political sponsors. Third, when compared to other models of bureaucratic behaviour the budget-maximizing thesis compares unfavourably. For example, Cope found the budget-maximizing model to be very weak at explaining how local authorities in Britain cut spending when compared to other models (1990; 1992; 1994).

Generally there are four weaknesses of the budget-maximizing thesis as a model of bureaucratic behaviour. First, the model assumes that bureaucrats are self-interested, but there is evidence that bureaucrats are 'mission-committed' (Margolis, 1975), and 'might actually care about the content of the policies they are enacting and implementing' (Goodin, 1982, p. 31). The interests of bureaucrats are shaped by organizational cultures and professional values, and consequently their self-interests are mediated by ideology. Second, even if bureaucrats are self-interested, budget-maximizing is not necessarily a successful strategy to maximize their utility. The utility of a bureaucrat is highly dependent on the function of the bureau, type of budget and rank of the bureaucrat (Dunleavy, 1991, pp. 147–248). For example, bureaucrats in finance departments generally seek to minimize budgets as part of their agency mission. The budget-maximizing model is far too generalized in presuming that all bureaucrats budget-maximize. Third, the budget-maximizing thesis assumes that the sponsor is weak, but sponsors do deploy resources to counter any budget-maximizing behaviour of bureaucrats. In their dealings with bureaucrats, for example, sponsors often possess statutory authority, employ advisers, and enjoy outside political support. Fourth, the budget-maximizing model assumes that the relationship between a sponsor and bureau constitutes a 'bilateral monopoly'. However, a government bureau often does not occupy a monopoly position in relation to its sponsor, as a bureau is increasingly in competition with other government and non-government agencies to provide a public service. As a result of these criticisms, the budget-maximizing thesis should be discarded as a plausible model of bureaucratic behaviour in favour of more sophisticated and empirically sound models. The bureau-shaping model is an attempt to overcome the problems encountered by the budget-maximizing model, though it too is part of the rational choice camp.

THE BUREAU-SHAPING MODEL DESCRIBED

The bureau-shaping model has been developed by Dunleavy (1985; 1989a; 1989b; 1991). The model attempts to overcome the major objections levelled at the budget-maximizing model. It represents a significant public choice reconstruction of bureaucratic behaviour. Dunleavy assumed still that bureaucrats 'are essentially instrumental, maximizing their personal utilities when making official decisions' (1985, p. 300). The model also serves as a critique of, as well as an alternative to, the budget-maximizing model. In contrast to Niskanen, Dunleavy argued that rational bureaucrats 'have few incentives to pursue budget-maximizing strategies' (1991, p. 174). He cited four reasons why bureaucrats are not simple budget-maximizers.

First, there exists collective action problems in pursuing budget-maximizing strategies, because budget-maximization is not 'a private good pursued by a hegemonic official' (Dunleavy, 1991, p. 175). Budget-maximization is a collective strategy requiring the co-operation of several actors. Dunleavy added:

> Any given bureaucrat has a range of both individual and collective strategies open for boosting her welfare. She can most directly and strongly improve her personal position using an individual strategy – for here a successful effort generates a pay-off which does not need to be shared with others. By contrast, with any collective strategy there is a more indirect and complex link between a successful outcome and a welfare boost for the individual …. An overall budget increase for the agency has particularly indeterminate implications for any official, however senior. Consequently, rational bureaucrats put their efforts primarily into individual utility-maximizing strategies. They only pursue collective goods strategies if other options are foreclosed or are already fully exploited. (1991, pp. 175–6)

Consequently a bureaucrat will pursue individual strategies (such as promotion) before pursuing collective strategies (such as budget-maximization). Furthermore, Dunleavy claimed the 'utility pay-offs from generalized budgetary increments are likely to vary, roughly inversely with rank' (1991, p. 178). He argued:

> Bottom-rank bureaucrats gain most from budget increases, but they also know that they can make virtually no difference to the outcome individually …. By contrast, officials at the top of the bureau can significantly affect outcomes, but stand to gain least from budgetary expansion, confront high advocacy costs in exercising their influence and have more opportunity to boost their welfare in alternative ways. (1991, p. 180)

Second, the extent to which the utility of bureaucrats corresponds with the size of budget 'varies greatly across different components of overall budgets, and across distinct types of agencies' (Dunleavy, 1991, p. 174). Consequently the strategies of bureaucrats, including budget-maximizing strategies, vary between budgets and agencies. Dunleavy identified four types of agency budget:

(1) the *core budget* consisting of 'those expenditures which are spent directly on its own operations (rather than going outside the agency in transfers, contracts or grants to other public sector bodies)' (1991, p. 181);

(2) the *bureau budget* comprising 'all core budget items above, plus any monies the agency pays out to the private sector, for example by awarding contracts to private firms, or by making transfer payments to individuals and firms, or by directly paying interest on capital debts' (1991, p. 181);

(3) the *program budget* including 'its bureau budget, plus any monies which the agency passes on to other public sector bodies for them to spend' (1991, p. 182); and,

(4) the *super-program budget* embracing 'the agency's program budget plus any spending by other bureaus from their own resources, over which the agency none the less either exercises some policy responsibilities, or which it can limit or expand in planning terms, or for which it can wholly or partially claim political credit (and hence also incur political blame)' (1991, p. 183).

Furthermore, Dunleavy argued the relative importance of these different types of budget varies between types of agency (1991, p. 183). He identified five basic and 'functionally defined' types of government agency (1991, p. 183):

(1) *delivery agencies* which 'directly produce outputs or deliver services to citizens or enterprises, using their own personnel to carry out most policy implementation' (1991, p. 183);

(2) *regulatory agencies* which 'limit or control the behaviour of individuals, enterprises or other bodies, using licensing systems, reporting controls, performance standards or some similar system' (1991, p. 184);

(3) *transfer agencies* which 'handle payments of some form of subsidy or entitlement by government to private individuals or firms' (1991, p. 184);

(4) *contracts agencies* which 'work on research and development into projects, drawing up equipment or service specifications, liaising with

companies, contract management and compliance, etc' (1991, p. 186); and,

(5) *control agencies* which 'channel funding to other public sector bureaus in the form of grants or inter-governmental transfers, and ... supervise how these other state organizations spend the money and implement policy' (1991, p. 186).

The bureau-shaping model thus differentiates between different types of budgets and agencies. For example, delivery agencies usually employ many staff to provide services, and consequently 'their core budgets absorb a high proportion of their bureau and program budgets' (Dunleavy, 1991, p. 184). Transfer agencies are 'money-moving organizations', and their core budgets 'should absorb a very low proportion of the bureau budget' (Dunleavy, 1991, p. 184). Bureaucrats pursue different strategies depending on the type of budget and type of agency.

Third, the conditions within which bureaucrats pursue budget-maximizing strategies varies with the rank of bureaucrat, type of budget, and type of agency. Dunleavy argued:

> The most basic individual utility gains from budget increases, and those which are most important for bottom- and middle-ranking officials, are all associated with the core budget. By contrast, the more diffuse utility gains from budgetary expansion, and those which are most important for top-ranking officials, are primarily linked to the bureau budget. (1991, p. 192)

As a result the incentive to pursue budget-maximizing strategies 'will be strongest in organizations where there is a close relationship between core, bureau and program budgets' (Dunleavy, 1991, p. 193). Rational bureaucrats will care less about 'whether the super-program budget spent by lower-tier agencies in their policy area increases or declines' (Dunleavy, 1991, p. 194). The budget-maximizing incentive will be found more in delivery agencies where 'the welfare of both senior and lower-ranking officials seems to be most closely tied to program budget increases' (Dunleavy, 1991, p. 193). Bureaucratic rank, budget-type and agency-type are thus important determinants of the utility-maximizing strategies deployed by rational bureaucrats.

Fourth, the bureau-shaping model assumes the motivations of bureaucrats are more varied than that assumed in the budget-maximizing model. Dunleavy wrote:

> ...there is a general presumption ... that senior managers put less stress than lower-ranking bureau members on the pecuniary or near-pecuniary

components of their utility function (such as income, job security, or perks). Instead, higher-ranked bureaucrats place more emphasis upon non-pecuniary utilities: such as status, prestige, patronage and influence, and most especially the interest and importance of their work tasks. (1991, p. 200)

Furthermore, given that public sector employment systems, compared to private sector employment systems, limit the extent to which bureaucrats can determine their remuneration, 'work-related utilities seem to be a major continuing influence on the ways in which officials behave within the public sector' (Dunleavy, 1991, p. 201). Consequently Dunleavy predicted:

Rational officials want to work in small, élite, collegial bureaus close to political power centres. They do not want to head up heavily staffed, large budget but routine, conflictual and low-status agencies. (1991, p. 202)

This four-fold critique of the budget-maximization model provides the essence of the bureau-shaping model. According to Dunleavy, rational bureaucrats 'concentrate on developing bureau-shaping strategies designed to bring their agency into line with an ideal configuration conferring high status and agreeable work tasks, within a budgetary constraint contingent on the existing and potential shape of the agency's activities' (1991, p. 209). The bureau-shaping model is more sophisticated than the budget-maximizing model because it differentiates between rank within a bureau, type of budget, type of agency, motivations of bureaucrats and type of utility-maximizing strategy pursued by bureaucrats.

THE BUREAU-SHAPING MODEL APPLIED

This section seeks to apply the bureau-shaping model in order to assess whether it possesses any explanatory power. Three applications of the model will be undertaken, using examples drawn from subnational, national and supranational governance. The bureau-shaping model will be tested by examining in detail how British local authorities make spending cuts, and in less detail, by investigating how executive agencies were established within British central government and by interpreting the role of the European Commission in the processes of economic and political integration within the EU.

Making Spending Cuts in British Local Government

Even before the IMF Crisis of 1976, Tony Crosland, the then Secretary of State for the Environment, announced to local authorities: 'The party's over' (Crosland, 1982, p. 295).

Spending cuts have been consistently on the local government agenda for nearly two decades. Since 1979 the Conservative government has attempted to cut local government spending, and has imposed many spending controls upon local authorities. However, despite these controls, local government spending has increased both in cash and real terms. The Thatcherite attack on local government spending failed. The Thatcher government, unlike the preceding Callaghan government, failed to extract wholesale cuts from local authorities. Nevertheless, though there have been no cuts in the whole of local government spending, there have been cuts in the parts of local government spending, for example, capital projects and housing. Furthermore, the Conservative government's attempts to control the spending of local authorities applied a brake to their spending. Since the mid-1970s, and especially since the late 1970s, cutback management has been and remains a vogue concern in British local government.

In developing the bureau-shaping model, Dunleavy assumed the policies of an agency 'are set by bureaucrats interacting with their sponsor body' (1985, p. 300). He outlined five basic types of government agency, but conceded that classifying agencies by type is 'complicated' (1989a, p. 262). Agencies may perform more than one function, and thus display characteristics of more than one agency type. Stoker claimed local authorities 'are predominantly delivery agencies' (1991, p. 244). However, it is important to 'decompose officially unified organizations into components consisting of the different agency types ... , which are themselves functionally defined' (Dunleavy, 1991, p. 183). Stoker's description is insufficiently disaggregated, because a local authority can be further sub-divided into departments which can be classified by agency type. Departments manage budgets, implement policy and are overseen generally by an elected council (and its committees). They thus constitute agencies, with the council performing the sponsor role. A four-fold set of cutback management traits can be deduced from the bureau-shaping model relating to the strategies pursued by bureaucrats, different types of budgets and agencies, conditions for budget-maximizing, and motivations of bureaucrats.

First, the bureau-shaping model argues that the strategies pursued depend on the rank of bureaucrats. Bureaus are 'rank-structured environments' (Dunleavy, 1991, p. 174). Downs noted that the concept of monolithic bureaus 'is largely a myth' (1967, p. 133). The model would assume that local authority departments consist of bureaucrats of different ranks dominated by neither a chief officer nor a tightly-knit leadership team. Local authority departments are hierarchically arranged with officers ranked within departments, though officers enjoy considerable professional autonomy, and recent managerial reforms (such as compulsory competitive tendering) have challenged traditional hierarchical departmental structures. Generally a local authority department can be regarded as a loosely structured collection of ranked bureaucrats.

The bureau-shaping model posits that whether individual or collective strategies are pursued by bureaucrats depend on rank. Budget-maximizing is a collective strategy requiring 'concerted action by a number of officials' (Dunleavy, 1991, p. 175). Dunleavy claimed the benefits of budget increases are distributed 'more or less inversely to rank positions', whereby 'those at the bottom gain most, while those at the top gain least' (1985, p. 303). The model, therefore, would predict that the costs of budget reductions are borne more by lower-ranked than higher-ranked bureaucrats in local authorities. Indeed, higher-ranked bureaucrats are far more influential in formulating a cutback management strategy (Cope, 1992). They play a key role in making spending cuts and are sometimes rewarded for cutting spending; furthermore, they are more effective at resisting proposed spending cuts. For example, the contracting-out of service provision is a significant way of cutting local authority spending (Cope, 1995), which, according to Dunleavy, 'must be seen as a continuation of the strategies already well developed by senior policy-level bureaucrats for advancing their class (and frequently gender) interests against those of rank and file state workers and service consumers' (1986, p. 30). Lower-ranked bureaucrats are hurt more than higher-ranked bureaucrats when local authority spending is cut because they exercise less influence in making budgets.

Second, the bureau-shaping model distinguishes between four types of budget. Dunleavy noted that the idea of budget-maximizing behaviour 'is unilluminating until we can know precisely which elements of agency expenditure rational officials seek to boost' (1991, p. 181). The strategies adopted by bureaucrats in an agency will vary between type of budget – core budget (running expenses), bureau budget (core budget plus payments to private sector), program budget (bureau budget plus monies given to other public sector bodies), and super-program budget (program budget plus spending by other agencies significantly controlled by the agency). However, there are significant problems in operationalizing this budget typology. Dunleavy assumed the definition and measurement of a budget is a relatively non-problematic measure. Budgets are neither easy to define nor easy to measure. Following Larkey and Smith:

> Government budgets are premised on forecasts of revenues and expenditures. These forecasts are subject to both stochastic error and strategic manipulation. (1989, p. 123)

Budgets are political constructs and represent negotiated settlements between a coalition of actors. Budgeting is far more than an accounting exercise (Lehman and Tinker, 1987). The bureau-shaping model distinguishes between the four different types of budget depending on who receives budget monies. However, local authority budgets often do not state whether the local authority, private sector or another public sector body is to receive the budgeted monies, making it extremely difficult to apportion monies between different budget categories. For example, Dunleavy argued capital spending is part of an agency's bureau budget and not its core budget because 'contracts for this are assumed to go to private construction firms or other contractors' (1985, p. 307), but this assumption is far from valid as many local authorities employ their own workers to build capital projects.

The bureau-shaping model identifies five functionally defined types of agency. Dunleavy argued that the 'relative sizes of core, bureau and program budget levels fluctuate systematically across agencies' (1991, p. 183). The model would suggest that the strategies to cut spending will correspond with the type of agency. Local authorities have developed historically to provide public services (such as education, housing and social services), and their departments can be regarded generally as delivery agencies. However, not all local authority departments are delivery agencies, and not all bureaucrats within service departments are engaged in the delivery of public services. For example, central departments (such as finance and personnel) are servicing agencies, and service departments increasingly regulate other agencies (for example, private residential homes), transfer monies (such as housing benefit), award contracts (for example, refuse collection), and control other public sector bodies (for example, other local authorities in receipt of grant monies). Consequently classifying local authority departments by agency type is not straightforward.

Third, the bureau-shaping model states that budget-maximizing strategies are dependent upon rank of bureaucrat, type of budget, and type of agency. Dunleavy claimed that lower-ranking bureaucrats are more likely to defend the core budget, whereas higher-ranking bureaucrats defend the bureau budget of their agency. The model holds that different bureaucrats in different agencies seek to protect different budgets. Generally, the more powerful bureaucrats tend to deflect the axe to cut spending onto budgets defended by less powerful actors in the budget process. For example, local authorities tend to export spending cuts to other agencies, and thus protect their core budgets (Cope, 1994). Furthermore, budgets of service departments tend to be cut proportionately less than those of central departments in local government (Cope, 1994). The bureau-shaping model predicts that budget-maximizing is more likely to be found in delivery agencies where there is a close relationship between types of budget. Given nearly all departments in local authorities are essentially delivery agencies, the model would premise that local authority bureaucrats are more likely to pursue budget-maximizing strategies. However, though bureaucrats seek to protect and even boost their budgets, there is little evidence that the making of spending cuts in local government closely corresponds to the budget-maximizing model (Cope, 1994). Bureaucrats in service departments advocating spending are countered by bureaucrats in finance departments guarding revenues and ruling politicians making policy (Cope, 1992, pp. 52–4).

Fourth, the bureau-shaping model suggests that lower-ranked bureaucrats are motivated more by pecuniary gain than higher-ranked bureaucrats. Given the constraints of public sector employment systems, senior bureaucrats will find budget-maximizing 'a remarkably frustrating activity' (Dunleavy, 1991, p. 201). Instead they pursue bureau-shaping strategies to maximize their utility. Dunleavy argued that 'rational bureaucrats oriented primarily to work-related utilities pursue a bureau-shaping strategy designed to bring their bureau into a progressively closer approximation to "staff" (rather than "line") functions, a collegial atmosphere and a central location' (1991, pp. 202–3). Bureau-shaping strategies are pursued within externally imposed constraints. The bureau-shaping model would predict that within limits set by the council, senior bureaucrats seek to change the role of their department away from relatively low-status tasks like providing services to more high-status tasks like planning and regulating services. There is much evidence, particularly with the advent of compulsory competitive tendering and contracting-out, that many local authorities 'appear to be well along the path leading from direct provision to enabling authorities' (Biggs and Dunleavy, 1995b, p. 24). However, this shift is taking place mainly because of central government intervention and only partly because of strategies deployed by senior bureaucrats in local authorities.

Establishing Executive Agencies in British Central Government

Since the late 1980s British central government has been significantly transformed, mainly as a result of the Conservative government's Next Steps programme that established executive agencies (Jones, 1989). Campbell and Wilson believed that the programme 'promised (or threatened) to change the Whitehall model fundamentally' (1995, p. 45). On launching the Next Steps programme, the Ibbs Report stated:

> The aim should be to establish a quite different way of conducting the business of government. The central Civil Service should consist of a

relatively small core engaged in the function of servicing Ministers and managing departments, who will be the sponsors of particular government policies and services. Responding to these departments will be a range of agencies employing their own staff, who may or may not have the status of Crown servants, and concentrating on the delivery of their particular service, with clearly defined responsibilities between the Secretary of State and the Permanent Secretary on the one hand and the Chairmen or Chief Executives of the agencies on the other. (Jenkins et al., 1988, p. 15)

It recommended that agencies should be established to carry out much of the work previously done within government departments. It envisaged a civil service whereby a small number of senior civil servants would continue to advise ministers on policy matters, but the remaining civil servants would administer policy within agencies. The sponsoring government department would formulate policy which agencies administer and set agency budgets. The Ibbs Report was welcomed by the Conservative government, which planned a rolling programme of establishing agencies within central government. Dowding observed:

With the exception of wartime, never has the civil service changed so rapidly. Within three years of the start of Next Steps over 50 per cent of civil servants had moved into agencies and by the end of 1994 nearly 62 per cent of civil servants had done so with a further 17 per cent in jobs which are likely candidates for agency status. (1995, p. 105)

By April 1996, 125 executive agencies had been established, embracing over 382 000 civil servants (that is, over 70 per cent of all civil servants employed in government). The Next Steps programme 'set in motion enormous organizational and ... constitutional changes', by establishing the agencification of central government (Jordan and O'Toole, 1995, p. 3). As a result, the management of the civil service 'has now passed largely out of the hands of the mandarins into those of agencies and contracted-out bodies' (Kemp, 1994, p. 594), with senior civil servants primarily concerned with policy work supporting ministers.

The Next Steps programme is part of the new public management wave crashing through most Western governments, as it separates 'steering from rowing', thus leaving the centre to steer while other agencies row (Osborne and Gaebler, 1992, p. 34). It reinforces the increasing division between the core executive and the rest of central government. The core executive includes 'all those organizations and structures which primarily serve to pull together and integrate central government policies, or act as final arbiters within the executive of conflicts between different elements of the government machine' (Dunleavy and Rhodes 1990, p. 4). It comprises formal and informal structures and networks, such as the Prime Minister, cabinet committees and the Treasury. Under the Conservative government, its policy making capacity has been enhanced, with the rest of central government transformed increasingly to execute policies made and co-ordinated by the core executive.

The bureau-shaping model has been applied to explain the Next Steps programme. Dunleavy noted that its 'hiving-off proposals provide senior bureaucrats with a unique opportunity to engage in wholesale reshaping of their bureaus to attain their ideal form of small, élite, staff agencies' (1991, p. 226). He added:

> In the bureau-shaping model rational senior bureaucrats do not value routine, conflictual work in large organizations staffed mainly by non-élite personnel, exposed to public criticism and risks from mistakes and situated a long way from political power centres. (1991, p. 237)

Consequently the bureau-shaping model predicts that senior civil servants would favour the Next Steps programme, because it would release them from low-status tasks of managing staff and providing public services and would allow them to concentrate on high-status tasks of advising ministers and planning public services. Indeed, the relatively smooth implementation of the Next Steps programme indicates that it encountered little resistance from within the civil service. Resistance to the programme mainly came from the Treasury, which was concerned that its control over public expenditure and government personnel would be weakened because of the increased managerial autonomy enjoyed by agencies (Dunleavy, 1991, p. 226). Some resistance came from junior civil servants working in agencies, who 'feel that their job security has been lowered, the level of work they are expected to do has risen and there has not been any compensating pay rise' (Dowding, 1995, p. 106). However, senior civil servants largely embraced the establishment of executive agencies in central government, even the chief executives of agencies who 'prefer to feel that they are their own bosses' (though resenting 'excessive interference from the parent departments') (Dowding, 1995, p. 105). The Next Steps programme presented opportunities to senior civil servants to re-configure their departments away from the delivery of public services, thus making 'a convincing case' for the bureau-shaping model (Parsons, 1995, p. 317).

Understanding the European Commission in the European Union

On 1 November 1993 the Treaty on European Union came into effect, thus establishing the EU. The Maastricht Treaty represents an integrationist blueprint, consolidating disparate processes of economic and political integration that were taking place within the European Community (EC) since the mid-1950s (Carr and Cope, 1994). The EU comprises three pillars – the EC, Common Foreign and Security Policy (CFSP) and Justice and Home Affairs (JHA). The European Commission performs executive and bureaucratic functions within the EC. It employs under 20 000 staff mainly located in Brussels. It is headed by the College of Commissioners, consisting of twenty Commissioners (including its President) appointed by governments of the fifteen member states. Though obliged formally to be independent, Commissioners are 'national champions who defend national positions in the Commission' because they are appointed by and maintain close links with their national governments (Ludlow, 1991, p. 90). Its President, currently Jacques Santer, allocates policy portfolios between Commissioners, after considerable informal pressure from national governments and Commissioners. There are twenty-three directorates-general reporting to the responsible Commissioners. The role of the Commission is broadly two-fold; it initiates policy, and it oversees the implementation of policy.

First, as policy initiator, the Commission puts forward proposals for decision to the Council of Ministers, the EU's main decision making body consisting of fifteen political representatives drawn from member states. The formal power of policy initiation allows the Commission to control the policy-making agenda (Peters, 1994). The Council of Ministers can only amend a proposal with the agreement of the Commission, or if without its agreement, by acting unanimously. No decision can be made in the EC without first being drafted by the Commission. However, the Council of Ministers can request the Commission to draw up proposals for its deliberation. Moreover, the European Commission does not generally put forward proposals if there is little chance of them being accepted by the Council of Ministers. Consequently, it consults very widely with national governments, interest groups and others before drafting proposals to ensure their political feasibility. The European Commission is consequently a key actor in the process of engrenage reflecting the growing bureaucratic interpenetration between the Commission and government officials of member states (Peterson, 1995). Following Wallace, 'despite the attempts by governments to set up gatekeeping mechanisms, transnational networks of policy-making elites have emerged and become increasingly significant' (1983, p. 77).

Second, as overseer of policy implementation, the Commission does not implement many policies itself but supervises their implementation by national governments. It is very dependent upon member states for implementing policy, and as a result, there are often many implementation gaps where national governments are unable or unwilling to implement policy. The Commission is responsible for ensuring that EC law, which is binding upon member states, is observed. If not, it can refer matters to the Court of Justice and impose fines in certain cases.

Given its bureaucratic and executive functions, the Commission is more powerful than a traditional civil service because of its powers to initiate policy, and less powerful because of its lack of powers to implement policy. Generally the Commission cannot be regarded as a set of delivery agencies as it delivers little policy; rather it must be seen as a mix of regulatory, transfer and control agencies. Its core budget is a relatively small component of its overall budget, which is dominated by its program and super-program budgets (including the budget of the Common Agricultural Policy (CAP) that accounts for about one-half of the EC's budget). The European Commission corresponds closely with the ideal type of agency within which, the bureau-shaping model assumes, senior bureaucrats prefer to work. It has played a leading, and arguably increasing, role in the processes of integration within the EU (Nugent, 1995; Ross, 1995). From the CAP to the single currency and from the common market to single market, the Commission has been a key actor in extending the policy responsibilities of the EU. This Brussels-based bureaucratic élite has furthered the process of 'Europeanization' affecting all national governments belonging to the EU.

However, the privileged status of the Commission has come under attack periodically since the EC was formed in the 1950s. From the outset the Commission was intended to be the supranational policy-making body of the EC. But in the mid-1960s the French government challenged this interpretation of the Commission's role, and walked out of the EC until it received assurances from other member states (known as the Accords de Luxembourg) that a member state could veto the Commission's proposals to the Council of Ministers if their perceived vital interests are threatened. As a result, the Council of Ministers, not the Commission, became the dominant policy-making body of the EC. In the early 1990s there was another concerted attack, led by the British government, upon the power of the Commission. The outcome of this attack was formalized in the Maastricht Treaty which established the three pillars of the EU and endorsed the principle of subsidiarity.

The Commission's role is effectively sidelined in the two new pillars of CFSP and JHA, which are to be run as intergovernmental pillars dominated by national governments and not as supranational pillars mediated by the Commission. The legally binding principle of subsidiarity restricts the Commission to act in only those areas where national governments alone are unable to effectively act, thus trimming its power. The role of the Commission, as a supranational institution relatively detached from national pressures, has been challenged by national governments, many of which prefer to strike intergovernmental bargains and veto the Commission's proposals. As a result the role of the Commission has moved away from the ideal role assumed by the bureau-shaping model.

THE BUREAU-SHAPING MODEL EVALUATED

The above applications of the bureau-shaping model reveal significant implications for the model's validity. According to Gamble, the bureau-shaping model is a 'highly influential' public choice contribution to the understanding of politics (1995, p. 529). Similarly, Radcliffe believed the model represented perhaps the 'most promising' British application of public choice theory (1991, p. 41). However, despite this acclaim, there are several criticisms and reservations that can be levelled against the bureau-shaping model that need to be countered in its future development. This section outlines three limitations of the bureau-shaping model relating to its explanatory power, methodological problems encountered in its application, and its assumptions.

First, as a deductive model, the bureau-shaping model claims to possess predictive power, and consequently its claims need to be empirically tested to assess its explanatory power. On rational choice models generally, Green and Shapiro wrote:

> On the one hand, great strides have been made in the theoretical elaboration of rational actor models. Formidable analytical challenges have attracted a number of first-class minds; rational choice theories have grown in complexity and sophistication as a result. On the other hand, successful empirical applications of rational choice models have been few and far between. (1994, p. ix)

They argued that the systematic examination of rational choice theory 'reveal the emperor to be, if not entirely naked, somewhat scantily clad' (1994, p. 180). If bureau-shaping is to progress from a model simplifying to a theory explaining a complex reality, then its applications need to provide evidence of empirical fit. From the three applications of the bureau-shaping model described in the previous section, it is clear there is some empirical fit. In making spending cuts in British local government, senior bureaucrats are sensitive to the type of budget being cut and attempt to reshape their agencies away from the delivery of services. The Next Steps programme, establishing executive agencies in British central government, allows senior bureaucrats to concentrate more on making policy by advising politicians and less on administering policy by managing staff. The European Commission, as the bureaucratic arm of the EU, enjoys a central role in formulating policy, while only indirectly getting involved in its administration. However, the bureau-shaping model is a supply-side rational choice model attempting to explain how bureaucrats supply what politicians demand. Consequently, it provides an incomplete account of how public services are produced in governments. The model cannot explain the demand for public services that is supplied by bureaucrats. The bureau-shaping model is 'strangely non-political' (Radcliffe 1991, p. 41), because, by definition, it ignores the role of political parties, legislatures, government ministers and interest groups in shaping the demand for public services. For example, local authority bureaucrats generally framed their advice on where to cut spending within the preferences of the ruling local politicians. The Conservative government was fully committed to establishing agencies in central government, and consequently, any resistance from senior bureaucrats was never likely to succeed, possibly pushing them to acquiesce to rather than support for implementing the Next Steps programme. The expansionist plans of the European Commission were often trimmed and thwarted by national governments, as they wanted to assert control over the policy process in the EU. These limitations of the bureau-shaping model suggest that, as a supply-side model, it needs to be complemented by demand-side models in order to fully explain the behaviour of bureaucrats and the political environment within which they work. As James noted, senior bureaucrats 'are constrained by the actions of politicians' (1994, p. 343).

Second, there are considerable, and possibly insurmountable, difficulties in operationalizing the bureau-shaping model. More generally, Green and Shapiro noted that 'empirical applications of rational choice theory in political science since the 1960s have been marred by a syndrome of methodological shortcomings' (1994, p. 202). There are two principal methodological problems in applying the bureau-shaping model relating to its requirement to distinguish between agency-type and budget-type. Dunleavy distinguished between five basic types of government agency – namely, delivery, regulatory, transfer, contracts and control agencies – though he listed taxing, trading and servicing agencies as additional agency-types. He argued that these 'main analytic' types of agency created 'an exhaustive typology' (1989a, pp. 254–5), though later the typology also included super-control agencies that 'resemble control agencies ... [but] ... channel monies not to bureaus at other (lower) tiers of government, but to other bureaus forming part of the same tier of administration' (Biggs and Dunleavy, 1995b, p. 13). However, Dunleavy never explicitly stated the criteria used to identify these functionally defined agency-types. His typology does not include the whole gamut of different bureaucratic agencies, and excludes those performing representation/advocacy and adjudication functions. Furthermore, a government agency often shares characteristics of more than one agency-type. A British local authority is a delivery, regulatory, transfer, contracts, control, super-control, taxing, trading and servicing agency. Though Dunleavy argued that an agency should be sub-divided into its constituent functionally defined parts, one part of an agency may still possess characteristics of more than one agency type. For example, an education department of a British local authority is a delivery, regulatory, contracts, control and super-control agency. There are problems classifying agencies into functionally defined types because agencies often perform more than one function, and as a result the bureau-shaping model involves 'a fairly high level of aggregation' (Smith et al., 1993, p. 576).

There are also problems classifying budgets between budget types. Dunleavy distinguished between the core, bureau, program and super-program budget, though later he added the folio budget that 'includes monies which the agency controls but passes on to other agencies at the same tier of government' (Biggs and Dunleavy, 1995a, p. 688). The addition of the folio budget to the budget typology facilitates agency disaggregation. However, this typology is information hungry, requiring considerable data on budgeted monies and their recipients. Much of this data is not documented by agencies in their annual reports, budget reports, and so on. In a study of the Department of Social Security, James noted that the 'information required for a full testing of the bureau-shaping model ... is unavailable' (1995b, p. 624). By distinguishing between agency-type and budget-type, the bureau-shaping model is more sophisticated than the budget-maximizing model but its greater sophistication create difficulties in operationalizing the model.

Third, the bureau-shaping model is a deductive model based on a certain set of assumptions. In particular, it assumes that the utility of senior bureaucrats is 'derived from the core budget' which contains monies that can be used 'to obtain perks for themselves', such as salaries and 'pleasant offices'; and that their utility is 'derived from proportion of policy work time' which 'is liked because it involves innovation, often entails working in small staff units and requires officials to have a close proximity to political power sources such as ministers' (James, 1994, p. 341). These relatively parsimonious assumptions are merely asserted in the bureau-shaping model, and are not subject to empirical scrutiny. Green and Shapiro commented that 'all explanations rest on simplifying abstractions that distort reality', but the parsimony of rational choice theory may further distort 'reality' (1994, p. 191). The bureau-shaping model makes 'simple assumptions about the preferences of individual actors and the institutional environment in which they operate' (James, 1995b, p. 629). These assumptions, though perhaps intuitively reasonable, are 'open to question' (Radcliffe, 1991, p. 42), and need to be empirically tested as there 'is no way to find out which assumptions in explanatory models are casually pertinent absent empirical testing' (Green and Shapiro, 1994, p. 192). Though the bureau-shaping model's hard-edged motives of bureaucrats lend themselves more to quantitative analysis, they may not represent their actual motives which may be far more 'complex' (and less quantifiable) than the bureau-shaping model assumes (Schein, 1988, p. 38).

In conclusion, the bureau-shaping model represents a significant theoretical advance, particularly when compared to its budget-maximizing antecedent. By distinguishing between bureaucratic rank, agency-type and budget category, the model offers valuable insights into the workings of bureaucracy as demonstrated by its partial empirical fit when applied. However, it needs to be applied further, particularly in countries other than Britain. It may be that the relatively peculiar bureaucratic culture of Britain makes the bureau-shaping model redundant elsewhere. Furthermore, the model needs to compared more systematically with other models of bureaucracy (especially with those drawn from outside the world of rational choice). The bureau-shaping model remains a fledgling model (as seen by its later refinements in light of its (so far) limited applications). Greater empirical application and theoretical comparison may lead to further refinements of the bureau-shaping model, thus enhancing its already significant explanatory power.

Bibliography

Alexander, M. and Young, D. (1996), 'Strategic Outsourcing', *Long Range Planning*, Vol. 29, 116–19.

Almond, G.A. (1991) 'Rational choice theory and the social sciences' in Monroe, K.R. (ed.) *The Economic Approach to Politics*, New York: HarperCollins.

Anderson J.J. (1991) 'Sceptical Reflections on a Europe of Regions', *Journal of Public Policy*, vol. 10, pp. 417–47.

Anderson, S. and Eliassen, K. (1991) 'European Community Lobbying', *European Journal of Political Research*, vol. 20, no. 2, pp. 173–87.

Anderson, S. and Eliassen, K. (1993) *Making Policy in Europe*, London: Sage.

Audit Commission (1991) *A Rough guide to Europe: Local Authorities and the EC*, London: HMSO.

Balme, R. and Le Gales, P. (1996): 'Stars and Black Holes: French Regions and Cities in the European Galaxy' in Goldsmith and Klaussen, 1996.

Barber, B. (1991) 'Democracy and Globalization' (Plenary Lecture to the UK Political Studies Association Annual Conference, Lancaster University).

Barzell, Y. (1989) *Economic Analysis of Property Rights*, Cambridge: Cambridge University Press.

Bell, D. (1974) *The Coming of Post-Industrial Society*, London: Heinemann.

Bennington, J. (1994) *Local Democracy and the European Union*, London: Commission for Local Democracy, Research Report no 6.

Berger, P.L. and Luckman, T. (1975) (first published 1966), *The Social Construction of Reality: a treatise on the sociology of knowledge*, Harmondsworth: Penguin books.

Biggs, S. and Dunleavy, P. (1995a) 'Changing organisational patterns in local government: a bureau-shaping analysis' in Lovenduski, J. and Stanyer, J (eds) *Contemporary Political Studies 1995: Volume Two*, Belfast: Political Studies Association of the United Kingdom.

Biggs, S. and Dunleavy, P. (1995b) 'Local Government Organization in a "Post-Bureaucratic" Age: a Bureau-Shaping Analysis' (paper presented to Joint Sessions of Workshops, European Consortium for Political Research, University of Bordeaux, 27 April–2 May).

Blais, A. and Dion, S. (eds) (1991) *The Budget-Maximizing Bureaucrat*, Pittsburgh: University of Pittsburgh Press.

Blore, I. (1987) 'Are local bureaucrats budget or staff maximizers?', *Local Government Studies* 13(3).

Boston, J. (1992) 'The limits to contracting out: The case of policy advice' (unpublished paper: University of Victoria, Wellington, New Zealand).

Cabinet Office (1991) *Improving Management in Government: The Next Steps Agencies – Review* 1991, Cm 1760, London: HMSO.

Cabinet Office (1994) *The Civil Service: Continuity and Change*, Cm 2627, London: HMSO.

Cabinet Office (1995) *The Civil Service: Taking Forward Continuity and Change*, CM 2748, London: HMSO.

Campbell, C. (1994) 'Reconciling Central Guidance and Managerialism: Conflicts Between Coherence and Discretion, the case of Whitehall', paper for XVth World Congress of IPSA, August, Berlin.

Campbell, C. and Wilson, G.K. (1995) *The End of Whitehall: Death of a Paradigm*, Cambridge, Mass. and Oxford: Blackwell publishers.

Carr, F. and Cope, S. (1994) 'Implementing Maastricht: the limits of European Union', *Talking Politics* 6(3).

Carver, T. and Thomas, P. (eds) (1995) *Rational Choice Marxism*, Basingstoke: Macmillan.

Chipperfield, Sir G. (1994) *The Civil Servant's Duty*, Essex Papers in Government, No. 95.

Coleman, J.S. and Fararo, T.J. (1992) 'Introduction' in Coleman, J.S. and Fararo, T.J. (eds) *Rational Choice Theory: Advocacy and Critique*, Newbury Park: Sage.

Competing For Quality (1991), London: HMSO, Cm 1730.

Cope, S. (1990) 'Cutback management in local government: an analytical framework', *Teaching Public Administration* 10(1).

Cope, S. (1992) 'Cutback management in local government: an empirical analysis', *Teaching Public Administration* 12(2).

Cope, S. (1994) 'Making spending cuts in local government: budget-maximising or bureau-shaping' in Dunleavy, P. and Stanyer, J. (eds) *Contemporary Political Studies 1994: Volume Two*, Belfast: Political Studies Association of the United Kingdom.

Cope, S. (1995) 'Contracting-out in local government: cutting by privatising', *Public Policy and Administration* 10(3).

Cooke, P. and Morgan, K. (1990) *Learning from Networking*, Regional Industrial Research Report no. 5, Cardiff.

Cox, A. (1993) *Public Procurement in the European Community: Volume I – The Single Market Rules and the Enforcement Regime after 1992*, Winteringham, South Humberside: Earlsgate Press.

Doig, A. (1995) 'Mixed Signals? Public Sector Change and the proper conduct of Public Business', *Public Administration*, Vol. 73, No. 2, pp. 191–212.

Crosland, S. (1982) *Tony Crosland*, London: Cape.

Domberger, S. and Hall, C. (1996) 'Contracting for Public Services: a review of antipodean experience', *Public Administration*, Vol. 74, No. 1, pp. 129–47.

Dowding, K.M. (1991) *Rational Choice and Political Power*, Aldershot: Edward Elgar.

Dowding, K. (1994a) 'The compatibility of behaviouralism, rational choice and "new institutionalism"', *Journal of Theoretical Politics* 6(1).

Dowding, K. (1994b) 'Policy communities: Don't stretch a good idea too far', in P. Dunleavy and J. Stanyer (eds) *Contemporary Political Studies 1994*, Belfast: UK Political Studies Association, Volume I, pp. 59–78.

Dowding, K. (1995) *The Civil Service*, London: Routledge.

Downs, A. (1967) *Inside Bureaucracy*, Boston: Little Brown.

Downs, G.W. and Larkey, P.D. (1986) *The Search for Government Efficiency*, Phililedphia: Temple.

Drewry, G. (1994) 'The Civil Service: from the 1940s to "Next Steps" and Beyond', *Parliamentary Affairs*, Vol. 47, No. 4.

Dunleavy, P. (1985) 'Bureaucrats, budgets and the growth of the state: reconstructing an instrumental model', *British Journal of Political Science* 15(3).

Dunleavy, P. (1986a) 'Explaining the privatization boom: public choice versus radical approaches', *Public Administration*, volume 64, no. 2, pp. 13–34.

Dunleavy, P. (1986b) 'The growth of sectoral cleavages and the stabilization of state expenditures', *Environment and Planning D: Society and Space*, volume 4, pp. 129–44.

Dunleavy, P. (1989a) 'The end of class politics?', in A. Cochrane and J. Anderson (eds) *Politics in Transition: Restructuring Britain*, London: Sage/Open University, pp.172–210.

Dunleavy, P. (1989b) 'The architecture of the British central state: Parts I and II', *Public Administration*, volume 67, nos 3 and 4, pp. 249–75 and 391–417.

Dunleavy, P. (1991) *Democracy, Bureaucracy and Public Choice*, Hemel Hempstead: Harvester Wheatsheaf; Englewood Cliffs, NJ: Prentice-Hall, 1992.

Dunleavy, P. (1992), 'Understanding the Structure of Public Sector Agencies' (Paper to the Australasian Political Studies Association Annual Conference, Australian National University, Canberra, September).

Dunleavy, P. (1993) 'The state', in R. Goodin and P. Pettit (eds) *Blackwell's Companion to Contemporary Political Philosophy*, Oxford: Blackwell, pp. 611–21.

Dunleavy, P. (1994) 'The Globalization of Public Services Production: Can Government be "Best in World"?', *Public Policy and Administration* Vol. 9, No. 2.

Dunleavy, P. and Hood, C. (1994) 'From Old Public Administration to New Public Management', *Public Money and Management*, pp. 9–16.

Dunleavy, P., King, D. and Margetts, H. (1996) 'Leviathon Bound: Bureaucracy and Budgeting in the American Federal State', unpublished book manuscript.

Dunsire, A. (1991) 'Bureaucrats and conservative governments' in Blais, A. and Dion, S. (eds) *The Budget-Maximizing Bureaucrat*, Pittsburgh: University of Pittsburgh Press.

Dunsire, A. (1995) 'Administrative theory in the 1980s: a viewpoint', *Public Administration* 73(1).

Dunsire, A. and Hood, C. (1989) *Cutback Management in Public Bureaucracies*, Cambridge: Cambridge University Press.

Elcock, H. (1991) *Public Administration: Change or Decay*, London: Longman.

Frissen, P. (1994) 'The Virtualization of Informatization of Public Administration', *Informatization and the Public Sector*, vol. 3, nos 3/4.

Fukuyama, F. (1992) *The End of History and the Last Man*, London: Penguin.

Gamble, A. (1995) 'The new political economy', *Political Studies* 43(3).

Garvey, G. 1992, *Facing the Bureaucracy: living and dying in a public agency*, San Francisco: Jossey Bass.

Gershuny, J. (1978) *After Industrial Society? The Emerging Self-Service Economy*, London: Macmillan.

Goldsmith, Sir J. (1995) *The Response: Gatt and Global free Trade*, Basingstoke: Macmillan.

Goldsmith, M. (1993) 'The Europeanisation of Local Government', *Urban Studies*, vol. 30, nos 4/5, pp. 683–700.

Goldsmith, M. and Klaussen, K. (eds) (1997): *European Integration and Local Government*, London: Edward Elgar.

Goldsmith, M. and Sperling, L. (1997): 'Local Government and the EU – the British Experience' in Goldsmith and Klaussen 1996.

Goldsworthy, D. (1991) *Setting Up Next Steps,* London: HMSO.

Gomez-Ibanez, J.A. and Meyer, J.R. (1993) *Going Private: The International Experience with Transport Privatization*, Washington DC: Brookings.

Goodin, R.E. (1982) 'Rational politicians and rational bureaucrats in Washington and Whitehall' *Public Administration* 60(1).

Gormley, W. (1989) *Taming the Bureaucracy: muscles, prayers, and other strategies*, Princeton: Princeton University Press.

Gray, J. (1993) *Beyond the New Right: markets, government, and the common environment*, London: Routledge.

Gray, J. (1996) 'To Cut a Long Tory Short', *Times Higher Education Supplement*, 15.3.96.

Green, D.P. and Shapiro, I. (1994) *Pathologies of Rational Choice Theory*, New Haven: Yale University Press.

Guba, E.G. (ed.) (1990) *The Paradigm Dialog*, London: Sage.

Hammer, M. and Champy, J. (1993) *Reengineering the Corporation*, Australia: Allen and Unwin.

Hart, D.K. (1989) 'A Partnership in Virtue Among All Citizens: The Public Service and Civic Humanism', *Public Administration Review*, 49 (101).

Hayek, F.A. (1948) *Individualism and Economic Order*, Chicago: Regency.

Heclo, H. (1978) 'Issue networks and the executive establishment' in King, A. (ed.) *The New American Political System*, Washington, DC: American Enterprise Institute for Public Policy Research.

Hirst, P. and Thompson, G. (1995) 'Globalisation and the Future of the Nation State', *Economy and Society*, Vol. 24, No. 3, pp. 408–42.

Hood, C. (1983) *The Tools of Government*, London: Macmillan.

Hood, C. (1990) *Beyond the Public Bureaucracy State? Public Administration in the 1990s*, London: LSEPS.

Hood, C. (1995) 'Contemporary Public Management: A New Global Paradigm?', *Public Policy and Administration*, Vol. 10, No. 2, pp. 104–17.

Hood, C., Huby, M. and Dunsire, A. (1984) 'Bureaucrats and budgeting benefits: how do British central government departments measure up?', *Journal of Public Policy* 4(3).

Hood, C. and Margetts, H. (1993) 'Informatization and public administration trends: Igniting, fuelling or dampening?' (Paper to the ESRC/PICT seminar on Public Sector Informatization, 10 December).

Hood, C. and Peters, B.G. (1994), *Rewards at the Top*, London: Sage.

Hughes, O.E. (1994), *Public Management and Administration: an introduction*, Basingstoke: Macmillan.

Ingraham, P. (1995) 'Reinventing the American Federal Government: Reform Redux or Real Change', Paper to the ESRC Public Service Seminar, LSE, February.

James, O. (1994) 'Explaining the Next Steps reorganisation in the Department of Social Security: an application of the bureau-shaping model', in Dunleavy, P. and Stanyer, J. (eds) *Contemporary Political Studies 1994: Volume One*, Belfast: Political Studies Association of the United Kingdom.

James, O. (1995a) 'The agency "revolution" in Whitehall: a bureau-shaping analysis', in Lovenduski, J. and Stanyer, J. (eds) *Contemporary Political Studies 1995: Volume One*, Belfast: Political Studies Association of the United Kingdom.

James, O. (1995b) 'Explaining the Next Steps in the Department of Social Security; the bureau-shaping model of central state reorganization' *Political Studies* 43(4).

James, S. (1992) *British Cabinet Government*, London: Routledge.

Jenkins, K., Caines, K. and Jackson, A. (1988) *Improving Management in Government: The Next Steps*, London: HMSO.

John, P. (1994a) 'UK sub-national offices in Brussels: diversification or regionalisation', ESRC Research Seminar, *British Regionalism and Devolution in a Single Europe*, London: LSE, May.

John, P. (1994b) *The Europeanisation of British Local Government: New Management Strategies*, Luton: LGMB.

Jones, G.W. (1989) 'A revolution in Whitehall? Changes in British central government since 1979', *West European Politics* 12(3).

Jordan, G. (1992) 'Next Steps Agencies: from Managing by Command to Managing by Contract?', *Aberdeen Papers in Accountancy, Finance and Management*, W6, Department of Accountancy.

Jordan, G. and O'Toole, B.J. (1995) 'The Next Steps: origins and destinations' in O'Toole, B.J. and Jordan, G. (eds) *Next Steps: Improving Management in Government?*, Aldershot: Dartmouth.

Kaufman, H. (1981) 'Fear of bureaucracy: a raging pandemic', *Public Administration Review*, vol. 41, no. 1, pp. 1–9.

Kay, J. (1993) *Foundations of Corporate Success*, Oxford: Oxford University Press.

Kelman, S. (1990) *Procurement and Public Management*, Washington, DC: American Enterprise Institute.

Kemp, Sir P. (1993) 'Beyond Next Steps,' Social Market Foundation Paper No. 17.

Kemp, P. (1994) 'The civil service White Paper: a job half finished', *Public Administration* 72(4).

Kettl, D. (1995) 'Building Lasting Reform', in D. Kettl and J. Dilulio Jr (eds) *Inside the Reinvention Machine*, Washington: Brookings.

Kettl, D. and Fesler, J. (1991) *The Politics of the Administrative Process*, New Jersey: Chatham House Publishers.

King, D.S. (1987) *The New Right: Politics, Markets and Citizenship*, Basingstoke: Macmillan.

Kuhn, T. (1970) (first published 1962), *The Structure of Scientific Revolutions*, Chicago: Chicago University Press.

Lancaster, K. (1974) *Introduction to Modern Microeconomics*, Chicago: Rand McNally.

Lane, J-E. (1993) *The Public Sector: Concepts, Models and Approaches*, London: Sage.

Lane, R E. (1983) 'Procedural goods in a democracy: how one is treated versus what one gets', *Social Justice Research*, Volume 2, pp. 177–92.

Lane, R.E. (1986) 'Market justice, political justice', *American Political Science Review*, vol. 80, no. 2, pp. 383–402.

Lane, R.E. (1991) *The Market Experience*, Cambridge: Cambridge University Press.

Larkey, P.D. and Smith, R.A. (1989) 'Bias in the formulation of local government budget problems', *Policy Sciences* 22(2).

Lawson, N. (1992) *The View from No 11*, London: Bantam.

Lehman, C. and Tinker, T. (1987) 'The "real" cultural significance of accounts', *Accounting, Organizations and Society* 12(5).

Light, P. (1993) *Monitoring Government: Inspectors General and the search for accountability*, Washington: Brookings.

Lindblom, C.E. (1979) 'Still Muddling Through', *Public Administration Review*; Vol. 39, No. 6, pp. 517–25.

Lindblom, C. (1977) *Politics and Markets: The World's Political-Economic Systems*, New York: Basic.

Ludlow, P. (1991) 'The European Commission' in R. Keohane and S. Hoffmann (eds) *The New European Community*, Boulder: Westview Press.

Margetts, H. (1994) 'The National Performance Review, the Clinton Presidency and the Future Shape of American Government, in P. Dunleavy and J. Stanyer, *Contemporary Political Studies*, Proceedings of PSA Annual Conference.

Margetts, H. (1995) 'The automated state', *Public Policy and Administration*, vol. 27, no. 2, pp. 88–103.

Margetts, H. and Dunleavy, P. (1994) 'Enhancing executive autonomy in central government systems: Comparing the National Performance Review and Next Steps' (Paper to the ECPR Annual Workshops, Madrid, 15 April).

Margetts, H. and Smyth, G. (eds) (1994) *Turning Japanese? Britain with a Permanent Party of Governnment*, London: Lawrence and Wishart.

Margolis, J. (1975) 'Comment', *Journal of Law and Economics* 18(3).

Marsh, D. and Rhodes, R.A.W. (eds) (1992) *Policy Networks in British Government*, Oxford: Clarendon Press.

Martin, S. and Pearce, G. (1994) 'The Impact of Europe on local government regional partnerships in local economic development' in Dunleavy, P. and Stanyer, J. (eds) *Contemporary Political Studies*, vol. 2, Exeter: PSA.

Marquand, D. (1994) 'Commentary', *Political Quarterly*, Vol. 65, no. 2.

Massey, A. (1993) *Managing the Public Sector; a comparative analysis of the United Kingdom and the United States*, Aldershot: Edward Elgar.

Massey, A. (1995a) 'Civil Service Reform and Accountability', *Public Policy and Administration*, Vol. 10, No. 1.

Massey, A. (1995b) 'Ministers, The Agency Model and Policy Ownership', *Public Policy and Administration*, Vol. 10, No. 2.

Massey, A. (1995c) *After Next Steps: an examination of the implications for policy making of the developments in executive agencies*, London: OPS, Cabinet Office.

Mayer, J.W. and Rowan, B. (1977) 'Institutionalized organizations: Formal structure as myth and ceremony', *American Journal of Sociology*, vol. 83, no. 2, pp. 440–63.

Mazey, S. and Richardson, J. (eds) (1993) *Lobbying in the European Community*, Oxford: Oxford University Press.

McGuire, T.G. (1981) 'Budget-maximizing governmental agencies: an empirical test', *Public Choice* 36(3).

Mellon, E. (1993) 'Executive Agencies: Leading Change from the Outside', *Public Money and Management*, Vol. 13, No. 2.

Mills, M. and Saward, M. (1994) 'All very well in practice, but what about the theory? A critique of the British idea of policy networks', in P. Dunleavy and J. Stanyer (eds) *Contemporary Political Studies 1994*, Belfast: UK Political Studies Association, Volume I, pp. 79–92.

Moe, R. (1992) *Reorganizing the Executive Branch in the Twentieth Century: Landmark Commissions*, Washington: Congressional Research Service, Library of Congress.

Moe, R. (1994) 'The "Reinventing Government" Exercise: Misinterpreting the Problem, Misjudging the Consequences', *Public Administration Review*, vol. 54 (March–April 1994), pp. 111–22.

Moe, T. (1984) 'The New Economics of Organization', *American Journal of Political Science*, 28 (733).

Moran, M. and Prosser, T. (1994) *Privatization and Regulatory Change in Europe*, Milton Keynes: Open University Press.

Mosher, F.C. (1968) *Democracy and Public Service*, New York: Oxford University Press.

Mulgan, R. (1989) *Democracy and power in New Zealand*, Auckland; Oxford University Press, Second edition.

National Audit Office (NAO) (1995a) *Department of Transport: Sale of DVOIT*, London: HMSO, HC 128.

National Audit Office (NAO) (1995a) *Inland Revenue: Market Testing the Information Technology Office*, London: HMSO, HC 245.

National Audit Office (NAO) (1995b) *The Banking Service provided by the Office of HM Paymaster General*, London: HMSO, HC 513.

National Performance Review (NPR) (1993) *From Red Tape to Results: Creating a Government that works better and costs less*, Report of the National Performance Review, Washington: GPO.

National Performance Review (NPR) (1994) *Status Report of the National Performance Review 1994*, Washington: GPO.

National Performance Review (NPR) (1995a) *Objectives, Principles, Approach: Phase II*, February 1995.

National Performance Review (NPR) (1995b) *Status Report of the National Performance Review 1995*, Washington: GPO.

Next Steps Review (1993) (Cm 2430), London: HMSO.

Next Steps Review (1994) (Cm 2750), London: HMSO.

Niskanen, W.A. (1971) *Bureaucracy and Representative Government*, New York: Aldine and Atherton.

Niskanen, W.A. (1973) *Bureaucracy: Servant or Master? Lessons from America*, London: Institute of Economic Affairs.

Niskanen, W.A. (1975) 'Bureaucrats and politicians', *Journal of Law and Economics* 18(3).

Niskanen, W.A. (1978) 'Competition among government bureaus', in Buchanan, J.M. et al., *The Economics of Politics*, London: Institute of Economic Affairs.

Niskanen, W.A. (1991) 'A reflection on Bureaucracy and Represen-tative Government', in Blais, A. and Dion, S. (eds) *The Budget-Maximizing Bureaucrat*, Pittsburgh: University of Pittsburgh Press.

Nugent, N. (1995) 'The leadership capacity of the European Commission', *Journal of European Public Policy* 2(4).

Office of Management and Budget (1993) *Information Resources Management Plan of the Federal Government*, Washington, DC: GPO.

Office of Management and Budget (OMB) (1994) *Making OMB More Effective in Serving the Presidency: Changes in OMB as a Result of the OMB 2000 Review*, Office Memorandum No. 94–16, Washington, DC: OMB.

Office of Public Service and Science (OPSS) (1993) *The Government's Guide to Market Testing*, London: HMSO.

O'Toole, B. (1989) '"The Next Steps" and Control of the Civil Service', *Public Policy and Administration*, Vol. 4, No. 1, pp. 41–51.

Osborne, D. and Gaebler, T. (1992) *Reinventing Government*, Reading, Mass.: Addison Wesley.

Oughton, J. (1994) 'Market Testing: The Future of the Civil Service', *Public Policy and Administration*, Vol. 9, No. 2.

Overman, E.S. and Boyd, K.J. (1994) 'Best practice research and Postbureaucratic Reform', *Journal of Public Administration Research and Theory*, Vol. 4, No. 1 67–83.

Parker, D. and Hartley, K. (1990) 'Competitive Tendering: Issues and Evidence', *Public Money and Management*, Vol. 10, No. 3.

Parsons, W. (1995) *Public Policy: an introduction to the theory and practice of policy analysis*, Aldershot: Edward Elgar.

Part, Sir A. (1990) *The Making of a Mandarin*, London: Andre Deutsch.

Peters, B.G. (1991) 'The European bureaucrat: the applicability of Bureaucracy and Representative Government to non-American settings' in Blais, A. and Dion, S. (eds) *The Budget-Maximizing Bureaucrat*, Pittsburgh: University of Pittsburgh Press.

Peters, B.G. (1994) 'Agenda-setting in the European Community', *Journal of European Public Policy* 1(1).

Peters, G. and Savoie, D. (1994) 'Reinventing Osborne and Gaebler', Canadian Centre for Management Development.

Peterson, J. (1995) 'Decision-making in the European Union: towards a framework for analysis', *Journal of European Public Policy* 2(1).

Pollitt, C. (1995) *Management techniques for the Public Sector: Pulpit and Practice*, Research Paper 17, Canadian Centre for Management Development.

Pressman, J. and Wildavsky, A. (1973) *Implementation*, Berkeley: University of California Press.

Quinn, J.B. (1992) *Intelligent Enterprise: A New Paradigm for a New Era*, New York: Macmillan.

Radcliffe, J. (1991) *The Reorganisation of British Central Government*, Aldershot: Dartmouth.

Rhodes, R.A.W. (1991) 'Theory and methods in British public administration: the view from political science', *Political Studies* 39(3).

Rhodes, R.A.W. (1994) 'The Hollowing out of the State', *The Political Quarterly*, Vol. 15, No. 2, pp. 138–51.

Rhodes R.A.W. (1995) 'The changing face of British public administration', *Politics* 15(2).

Richards, S. (1993) 'Editorial; Management of Change in the Civil Service', *Public Money and Management*, Vol. 13, No. 2.

Richards, S. and Rodrigues, J. (1993) 'Strategies for Management in the Civil Service: Change of Direction, *Public Money and Management*, Vol. 13, No. 2.

Roberts, P. (1994) 'The Role of Regions in the European Union', ESRC Research Seminar, British Regionalism and Devolution in a Single Europe, London: LSE.

Ross, G. (1995) *Jacques Delors and European Integration*, Cambridge: Polity Press.

Rostow, W.W. (1960) *The Stages of Economic Growth: A Non-Communist Manifesto*, Cambridge: Cambridge University Press.

Sabatier, P. and Jenkins-Smith, H. (eds) (1993) *Policy Change and Learning: An Advocacy Coalition Approach*, Boulder, Colorado: Westview.

Schein, E.H. (1988) *Organizational Psychology*, Englewood Cliffs: Prentice-Hall.

Sigelman, L. (1986) 'The bureaucrat as budget maximizer: an assumption examined', *Public Budgeting and Finance* 6(1).

Smith, A. (1776) *An Inquiry into the Nature and Causes of the Wealth of Nations*, London: Routledge, 1893.

Smith, M.J., Marsh, D. and Richards, D. (1993) 'Central government departments and the policy process', *Public Administration* 71(4).

Smith, T. (1996) 'Citizenship, Community and Constitutionalism', *Parliamentary Affairs*, Vol. 49, No.2.

Snellen, I. (1994) 'ICT: A Revolutionizing Force in Public Administration', *Informatization and the Public Sector* vol. 3, no. 3/4.

Stewart, J. (1992) *Accountability to the Public*, London: European Policy Forum.

Stewart, J. (1993) 'The limitations of government by contract', *Public Policy and Management*, Vol. 13, no. 3.

Stewart, J. and Walsh, K. (1992) 'Change in the Management of Public Services', *Public Administration*, Vol. 70, No. 4.

Stoker, G. (1991) *The Politics of Local Government*, Basingstoke: Macmillan.

Strassman, P. (1990) *The Business Value of Computers*, New Canaan, CT: Information Economics Press.

Taylor, J. (1992) 'Information Networking in Public Administration', *International Review of Administrative Sciences* vol. 58, no. 3.

Taylor, J. and Williams, H. (1991) 'From Public Administration to the Information Polity', *Public Administration* vol. 69, no. 2.

Tolchin, S.T. (1996) 'The Globalist from Nowhere: making governance competitive in the international environment', *Public Administration Review*, Vol. 56, No. 1, pp. 1–8.

Treasury and Civil Service Select Committee (1994) *The Role of the Civil Service Fifth Report*, London: HMSO, vol. 1.

Turpin, C. (1972) *Government Contracts,* Harmondsworth: Penguin Books.

Vogel, D. (1995) *Trading Up: Consumer and Environmental Regulation in a Global Economy*, Cambridge, Mass. and London: Harvard University Press.

Vowles, J. (1994) 'The politics of electoral reform in New Zealand', *International Journal of Political Research* (January).

Waldegrave, W. (1993a) *Public Service and the Future,* CPC, February.

Waldegrave, W. (1993b) 'The Reality of Reform and Accountability in Today's Public Service', Inaugural Public Finance Foundation/BDO Consulting Public Service Lecture.

Wallace, H. (1983) 'Negotiation, conflict, and compromise: the elusive pursuit of common policies' in Wallace, H., Wallace, W. and Webb, C. (eds) *Policy-Making in the European Community*, Chichester: Wiley.

Walzer, M. (1985) *Spheres of Justice: A Defence of Pluralism and Equality*, Oxford: Blackwell.

Ward, H. (1995) 'Rational choice theory', in Marsh, D. and Stoker, G. (eds) *Theory and Methods in Political Science*, Basingstoke: Macmillan.

Weber, M. (1946) *Essays on Bureaucracy*, Translated by Gerth and Mills, in Rourke, F. (ed.) (1986) *Bureaucratic Power in National Policy Making*, 4th edn, New York: Little Brown.

Weber, M. (1947) *The Theory of Social and Economic Organization*, Edinburgh: William Hodge, Translated by A.R. Henderson and T. Parsons.

Willcocks, L. and Fitzgerald, G. (1994) *A Business Guide to Outsourcing IT*, London: Business Intelligence.

Williamson, O. (1975) *Markets and Hierarchies: Analysis and Antitrust Implications*, New York: Free Press.

Williamson, O. (1985) *The Economic Institutions of Capitalism*, New York: Free Press.

Zifcak, S. (1989) *Administrative Reform in Whitehall and Canberra*, PhD thesis, London School of Economics.

Zifcak, S. (1994) *New Managerialism: Administrative Reform in Whitehall and Canberra*, Buckingham: Open University Press.

Index

Index by Auriol Griffith-Jones